HARCOURT
Science

Harcourt School Publishers

Orlando • Boston • Dallas • Chicago • San Diego

www.harcourtschool.com

The **blue and yellow macaw** (*Ara ararauna*) lives in the trees of the rain forest in South America and Central America. It can grow to be about 33 in. (84 cm) in length. It is the largest member of the parrot family. Its favorite food is the seed of the fruit of one rain forest tree. Blue and yellow macaws often gather at "lick" areas to eat mineral- and salt-bearing clay. The inside covers of this book show a closeup of blue and yellow macaw feathers.

Printed in the United States of America
ISBN 0-15-325383-5   UNIT A
ISBN 0-15-325384-3   UNIT B
ISBN 0-15-325385-1   UNIT C
ISBN 0-15-325386-X   UNIT D
ISBN 0-15-325387-8   UNIT E
ISBN 0-15-325388-6   UNIT F

10 11 12 032 10 09 08 07 06

Authors

Marjorie Slavick Frank
Former Adjunct Faculty Member
Hunter, Brooklyn, and
    Manhattan Colleges
New York, New York

Robert M. Jones
Professor of Education
University of Houston–
    Clear Lake
Houston, Texas

Gerald H. Krockover
Professor of Earth and Atmospheric
    Science Education
School Mathematics and
    Science Center
Purdue University
West Lafayette, Indiana

Mozell P. Lang
Science Education Consultant
Michigan Department
    of Education
Lansing, Michigan

Joyce C. McLeod
Visiting Professor
Rollins College
Winter Park, Florida

Carol J. Valenta
Vice President—Education, Exhibits,
    and Programs
St. Louis Science Center
St. Louis, Missouri

Barry A. Van Deman
Program Director, Informal Science
    Education
Arlington, Virginia

UNIT A LIFE SCIENCE

A World of Living Things

Unit Experiment   **A1**

CHAPTER 1 **Living Things**   **A2**

Lesson 1—What Are Cells? A4
Lesson 2—What Are Animals? A12
Lesson 3—What Are Plants with Seeds? A18
Lesson 4—What Are Fungi? A24
    Science Through Time • Discovering Cells A30
    People in Science • Gary Sayler A32
    Activities for Home or School A33
Chapter Review and Test Preparation A34

CHAPTER 2 **Animal Growth and Adaptations**   **A36**

Lesson 1—What Are the Basic Needs of Animals? A38
Lesson 2—How Do Animals' Body Parts Help Them Meet Their Needs? ...A46
Lesson 3—How Do Animals' Behaviors Help Them Meet Their Needs? A54
    Science and Technology • Robot Roaches and Ants A62
    People in Science • Jane Goodall A64
    Activities for Home or School A65
Chapter Review and Test Preparation A66

CHAPTER 3 **Plant Growth and Adaptations**   **A68**

Lesson 1—What Do Plants Need to Live? A70
Lesson 2—How Do Leaves, Stems, and Roots Help Plants Live? A76
Lesson 3—How Do Plants Reproduce? A82
    Science and Technology • Superveggies A88
    People in Science • Mary Agnes Meara Chase A90
    Activities for Home or School A91
Chapter Review and Test Preparation A92

CHAPTER 4 **Human Body Systems**   **A94**

Lesson 1—How Do the Skeletal and Muscular Systems Work? A96
Lesson 2—How Do the Respiratory and Circulatory Systems Work? A102
Lesson 3—How Do the Nervous and Digestive Systems Work? A108
    Science and Technology • Skin Adhesive A114
    People in Science • Rosalyn Sussman Yalow A116
    Activities for Home or School A117
Chapter Review and Test Preparation A118

Unit Expeditions   **A120**

UNIT B

LIFE SCIENCE
Looking at Ecosystems

Unit Experiment   **B1**

CHAPTER 1

Ecosystems   **B2**

Lesson 1—What Are Systems? B4
Lesson 2—What Makes Up an Ecosystem? B10
Lesson 3—What Are Habitats and Niches? B18
Lesson 4—What Are Tropical Rain Forests and Coral Reefs? B26
Lesson 5—What Are Some Saltwater Communities? B34
     Science and Technology • Computer Models of Ecosystems B42
     People in Science • Henry Chandler Cowles B44
     Activities for Home or School B45
Chapter Review and Test Preparation B46

CHAPTER 2

Protecting Ecosystems   **B48**

Lesson 1—What Kinds of Changes Occur in Ecosystems? B50
Lesson 2—How Do People Change Ecosystems? B58
Lesson 3—What Is Conservation? B66
     Science Through Time • National Parks B74
     People in Science • Ruth Patrick B76
     Activities for Home or School B77
Chapter Review and Test Preparation B78

Unit Expeditions   **B80**

UNIT C

EARTH SCIENCE
Earth's Surface

Unit Experiment   **C1**

CHAPTER 1

Earthquakes and Volcanoes   **C2**

Lesson 1—What Are the Layers of the Earth? **C4**
Lesson 2—What Causes Earthquakes? **C12**
Lesson 3—How Do Volcanoes Form? **C18**
     Science and Technology • Dante, Robot Volcano Explorer **C26**
     People in Science • Hiroo Kanamori **C28**
     Activities for Home or School **C29**
Chapter Review and Test Preparation **C30**

CHAPTER 2

Fossils   **C32**

Lesson 1—How Do Fossils Form? **C34**
Lesson 2—What Can We Learn from Fossils? **C40**
Lesson 3—How Do Fossil Fuels Form? **C50**
     Science Through Time • Buried in Time **C58**
     People in Science • Lisa D. White **C60**
     Activities for Home or School **C61**
Chapter Review and Test Preparation **C62**

Unit Expeditions   **C64**

UNIT D

EARTH SCIENCE

Patterns on Earth and in Space

Unit Experiment   **D1**

CHAPTER 1

Weather Conditions   D2

Lesson 1—What Makes Up Earth's Atmosphere? D4
Lesson 2—How Do Air Masses Affect Weather? D10
Lesson 3—How Is Weather Predicted? D18
    Science and Technology • Red Sprites, Blue Jets, and E.L.V.E.S. D24
    People in Science • Denise Stephenson-Hawk D26
    Activities for Home or School D27
Chapter Review and Test Preparation D28

CHAPTER 2

The Oceans   D30

Lesson 1—What Role Do Oceans Play in the Water Cycle? D32
Lesson 2—What Are the Motions of Oceans? D38
Lesson 3—What Is the Ocean Floor Like? D46
    Science and Technology • Deep Flight II D54
    People in Science • Rachel Carson D56
    Activities for Home or School D57
Chapter Review and Test Preparation D58

CHAPTER 3

Planets and Other Objects in Space   D60

Lesson 1—How Do Earth and Its Moon Move? D62
Lesson 2—How Do Objects Move in the Solar System? D68
Lesson 3—What Are the Planets Like? D74
Lesson 4—How Do People Study the Solar System? D82
    Science Through Time • Discovering the Planets D90
    People in Science • Clyde Tombaugh D92
    Activities for Home or School D93
Chapter Review and Test Preparation D94

Unit Expeditions   **D96**

UNIT E PHYSICAL SCIENCE
Matter and Energy

Unit Experiment   E1

CHAPTER 1

Matter and Its Changes   E2

Lesson 1—What Are Three States of Matter? E4
Lesson 2—How Can Matter Be Measured and Compared? E10
Lesson 3—What Are Some Useful Properties of Matter? E16
Lesson 4—What Are Chemical and Physical Changes? E24
    Science and Technology • Plastics You Can Eat. E32
    People in Science • Shirley Ann Jackson E34
    Activities for Home or School E35
Chapter Review and Test Preparation E36

CHAPTER 2

Heat—Energy on the Move   E38

Lesson 1—How Does Heat Affect Matter? E40
Lesson 2—How Can Thermal Energy Be Transferred? E46
Lesson 3—How Is Thermal Energy Produced and Used? E54
    Science and Technology • Refrigerants E60
    People in Science • Frederick McKinley Jones E62
    Activities for Home or School E63
Chapter Review and Test Preparation E64

CHAPTER 3

Sound   E66

Lesson 1—What Is Sound? E68
Lesson 2—Why Do Sounds Differ? E76
Lesson 3—How Do Sound Waves Travel? E82
    Science and Technology • Active Noise Control E90
    People in Science • Amar Gopal Bose E92
    Activities for Home or School E93
Chapter Review and Test Preparation E94

CHAPTER 4

Light   E96

Lesson 1—How Does Light Behave? E98
Lesson 2—How Are Light and Color Related? E108
    Science Through Time • Discovering Light and Optics E114
    People in Science • Lewis Howard Latimer E116
    Activities for Home or School E117
Chapter Review and Test Preparation E118

Unit Expeditions   E120

UNIT F

PHYSICAL SCIENCE
Forces and Motion

Unit Experiment   **F1**

CHAPTER 1 **Electricity and Magnetism**   **F2**

Lesson 1—What Is Static Electricity? F4
Lesson 2—What Is an Electric Current? F10
Lesson 3—What Is a Magnet? F16
Lesson 4—What Is an Electromagnet? F22
    Science Through Time • Discovering Electromagnetism F30
    People in Science • Raymond V. Damadian F32
    Activities for Home or School F33
Chapter Review and Test Preparation F34

CHAPTER 2 **Motion—Forces at Work**   **F36**

Lesson 1—What Is Motion? F38
Lesson 2—What Effects Do Forces Have on Objects? F44
Lesson 3—What Are Some Forces in Nature? F54
    Science and Technology • High-Speed Human-Powered Vehicles F60
    People in Science • Ellen Ochoa F62
    Activities for Home or School F63
Chapter Review and Test Preparation F64

CHAPTER 3 **Simple Machines**   **F66**

Lesson 1—How Does a Lever Help Us Do Work? F68
Lesson 2—How Do a Pulley and a Wheel and Axle Help Us Do Work? F76
Lesson 3—How Do Some Other Simple Machines Help Us Do Work? F82
    Science Through Time • Simple Machines and Water Transportation ..F90
    People in Science • Wilbur and Orville Wright F92
    Activities for Home or School F93
Chapter Review and Test Preparation F94

Unit Expeditions   **F96**

References Using Science Tools R2
    Health Handbook R7
    Using Science Reading Strategies R38
    Building a Science Vocabulary R44
    Glossary R50
    Index R60

Planning an Investigation

How do scientists answer a question or solve a problem they have identified? They use organized ways called **scientific methods** to plan and conduct a study. They use science process skills to help them gather, organize, analyze, and present their information.

Nathan is using this scientific method for experimenting to find an answer to his question. You can use these steps, too.

STEP 1 Observe, and ask questions.

- Use your senses to make observations.
- Record **one** question that you would like to answer.
- Write down what you already know about the topic of your question.
- Decide what other information you need.
- Do research to find more information about your topic.

What soil works best for planting marigold seeds?

I need to find out more about the different kinds of soils.

STEP 2 Form a hypothesis.

- Write a possible answer, or hypothesis, to your question. A **hypothesis** is a possible answer that can be tested.

- Write your hypothesis in a complete sentence.

My hypothesis is: Marigold seeds sprout best in potting soil.

STEP 3 Plan an experiment.

- Decide how to conduct a fair test of your hypothesis by controlling variables. **Variables** are factors that can affect the outcome of the investigation.

- Write down the steps you will follow to do your test.

- List the equipment you will need.

- Decide how you will gather and record your data.

I'll put identical seeds in three different kinds of soil. Each flowerpot will get the same amount of water and light. So, I'll be controlling the variables of water and light.

STEP 4 Conduct the experiment.

- Follow the steps you wrote.
- Observe and measure carefully.
- Record everything that happens.
- Organize your data so you can study it carefully.

I'll measure each plant every 3 days. I'll record the results in a table and then make a bar graph to show the height of each plant 21 days after I planted the seeds.

STEP 5 Draw conclusions and communicate results.

- Analyze the data you gathered.
- Make charts, tables, or graphs to show your data.
- Write a conclusion. Describe the evidence you used to determine whether your test supported your hypothesis.
- Decide whether your hypothesis was correct.

> Hmmm. My hypothesis was not correct. The seeds sprouted equally well in potting soil and sandy soil. They did not sprout at all in clay soil.

INVESTIGATE FURTHER

If your hypothesis was correct . . .

You may want to pose another question about your topic that you can test.

If your hypothesis was incorrect . . .

You may want to form another hypothesis and do a test of a different variable.

> I'll test this new hypothesis: Marigold seeds sprout best in a combination of clay, sandy, and potting soil. I will plan and conduct a test using potting soil, sandy soil, and a combination of clay, sandy, and potting soil.

Do you think Nathan's new hypothesis is correct? Plan and conduct a test to find out!

Using Science Process Skills

When scientists try to find an answer to a question or do an experiment, they use thinking tools called **process skills.** You use many of the process skills whenever you speak, listen, read, write, or think. Think about how these students use process skills to help them answer questions, do experiments, and investigate the world around them.

What Sarah plans to investigate

Sarah collects seashells on her visit to the beach. She wants to make collections of shells that are alike in some way. She looks for shells of different sizes and shapes.

Process Skills

Observe—use the senses to learn about objects and events.

Compare—identify characteristics of things or events to find out how they are alike and different.

Classify—group or organize objects or events in categories based on specific characteristics.

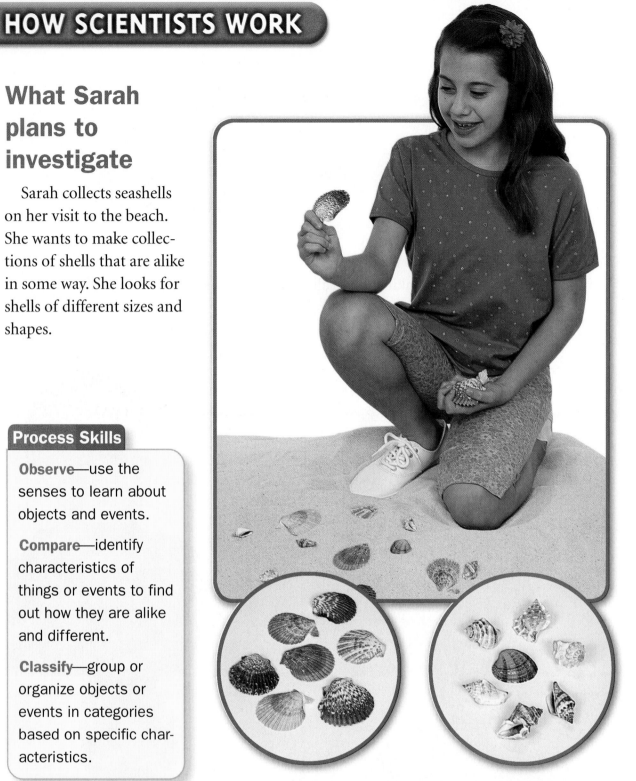

How Sarah uses process skills

She **observes** the shells and **compares** their sizes, shapes, and colors. She **classifies** the shells first into groups based on their sizes and then into groups based on their shapes.

What Ling plans to investigate

Ling is interested in learning what makes the size and shape of a rock change. He plans an experiment to find out whether sand rubbing against a rock will cause pieces of the rock to flake off and change the size or shape of the rock.

How Ling uses process skills

He collects three rocks, **measures** their masses, and puts the rocks in a jar with sand and water. He shakes the rocks every day for a week. Then he measures and **records** the mass of the rocks, the sand, and the container. He interprets his data and concludes that rocks are broken down when sand rubs against them.

Process Skills

Measure—Compare an attribute of an object, such as mass, length, or capacity, to a unit of measure, such as gram, centimeter, or liter.

Gather, Record, Display, or Interpret Data

► Gather data by making observations that will be useful for inferences or predictions.
► Record data by writing down the observations in a table, graph, or notebook.
► Display data by making tables, charts, or graphs.
► Interpret data by drawing conclusions about what the data shows.

Process Skills

Use a Model—make a representation to help you understand an idea, an object, or an event, such as how something works.

Predict—form an idea of an expected outcome, based on observations or experience.

Infer—use logical reasoning to explain events and draw conclusions based on observations.

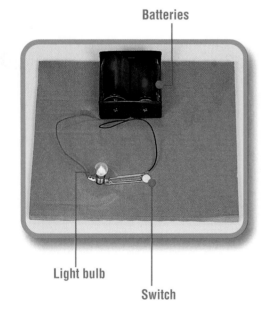

Batteries

Light bulb

Switch

What Justin plans to investigate

Justin wants to find out how the light switch in his bedroom works. He uses batteries, a flashlight bulb, a bulb holder, thumbtacks, and a paper clip to help him.

How Justin uses process skills

He decides to **use a model** of the switch and the wires in the wall. He **predicts** that the bulb, wires, and batteries have to be connected to make the bulb light. He **infers** that moving the paper clip interrupts the flow of electricity and turns off the light. Justin's model verifies his prediction and inference.

What Kendra plans to investigate

Kendra wants to know what brand of paper towel absorbs the most water. She plans a test to find out how much water different brands of paper towels absorb. She can then tell her father which brand is the best one to buy.

How Kendra uses process skills

She chooses three brands of paper towels. She **hypothesizes** that one brand will absorb more water than the others. She **plans and conducts an experiment** to test her hypothesis, using the following steps:

- Pour 1 liter of water into each of three beakers.
- Put a towel from each of the three brands into a different beaker for 10 seconds.
- Pull the towel out of the water, and let it drain back into the beaker for 5 seconds.
- Measure the amount of water left in each beaker.

Kendra **controls variables** by making sure each beaker contains exactly the same amount of water and by timing each step in her experiment exactly.

Reading to Learn

Scientists use reading, writing, and numbers in their work. They read to find out everything they can about a topic they are investigating. So it is important that scientists know the meanings of science vocabulary and that they understand what they read. Use the following strategies to help you become a good science reader!

Before Reading

- Read the **Find Out** statement to help you know what to look for as you read.
- Think: I need to find out what the parts of an ecosystem are and how they are organized.

- Look at the **Vocabulary** words.
- Be sure that you can pronounce each word.
- Look up each word in the Glossary.
- Say the definition to yourself. Use the word in a sentence to show its meaning.

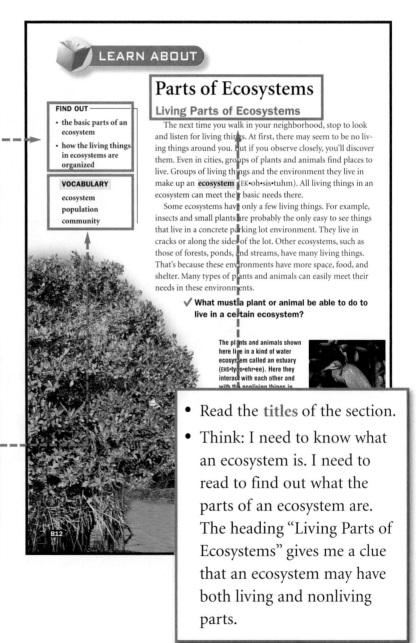

LEARN ABOUT

Parts of Ecosystems

Living Parts of Ecosystems

FIND OUT

- the basic parts of an ecosystem
- how the living things in ecosystems are organized

VOCABULARY

ecosystem
population
community

The next time you walk in your neighborhood, stop to look and listen for living things. At first, there may seem to be no living things around you. But if you observe closely, you'll discover them. Even in cities, groups of plants and animals find places to live. Groups of living things and the environment they live in make up an **ecosystem** (EK•oh•sis•tuhm). All living things in an ecosystem can meet their basic needs there.

Some ecosystems have only a few living things. For example, insects and small plants are probably the only easy to see things that live in a concrete parking lot environment. They live in cracks or along the sides of the lot. Other ecosystems, such as those of forests, ponds, and streams, have many living things. That's because these environments have more space, food, and shelter. Many types of plants and animals can easily meet their needs in these environments.

✔ What must a plant or animal be able to do to live in a certain ecosystem?

The plants and animals shown here live in a kind of water ecosystem called an estuary (EHS•tyoo•ehr•ee). Here they interact with each other and with the nonliving things in

B12

- Read the **titles** of the section.
- Think: I need to know what an ecosystem is. I need to read to find out what the parts of an ecosystem are. The heading "Living Parts of Ecosystems" gives me a clue that an ecosystem may have both living and nonliving parts.

During Reading

Find the **main idea** in the first paragraph.

- Groups of living things and their environment make up an ecosystem.

Find **details** in the next paragraph that support the main idea.

- Some ecosystems have only a few living things.
- Environments that have more space, food, and shelter have many living things.
- Plants and animals in an ecosystem can meet all their basic needs in their ecosystem.

Check your understanding of what you have read.

- Answer the question at the end of the section.
- If you're not sure of the answer, reread the section and look for the answer to the question.

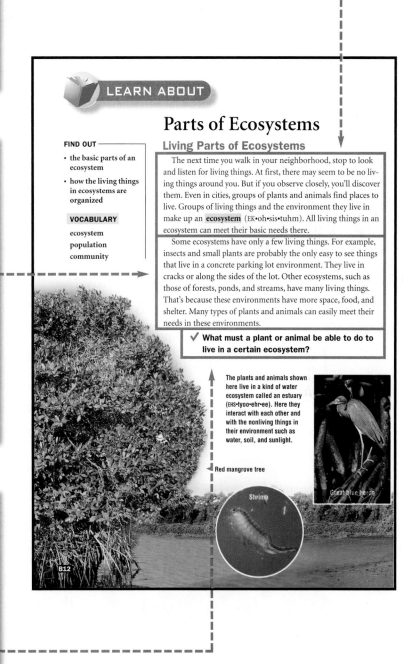

LEARN ABOUT

Parts of Ecosystems

Living Parts of Ecosystems

FIND OUT
- the basic parts of an ecosystem
- how the living things in ecosystems are organized

VOCABULARY

ecosystem
population
community

The next time you walk in your neighborhood, stop to look and listen for living things. At first, there may seem to be no living things around you. But if you observe closely, you'll discover them. Even in cities, groups of plants and animals find places to live. Groups of living things and the environment they live in make up an **ecosystem** (EK•oh•sis•tuhm). All living things in an ecosystem can meet their basic needs there.

Some ecosystems have only a few living things. For example, insects and small plants are probably the only easy to see things that live in a concrete parking lot environment. They live in cracks or along the sides of the lot. Other ecosystems, such as those of forests, ponds, and streams, have many living things. That's because these environments have more space, food, and shelter. Many types of plants and animals can easily meet their needs in these environments.

✓ What must a plant or animal be able to do to live in a certain ecosystem?

The plants and animals shown here live in a kind of water ecosystem called an estuary (EHS•tyoo•ehr•ee). Here they interact with each other and with the nonliving things in their environment such as water, soil, and sunlight.

Red mangrove tree

Shrimp

Great blue heron

B12

After Reading

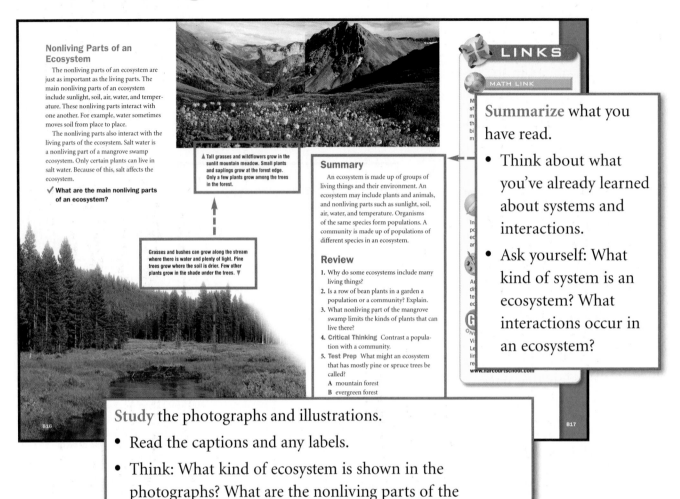

Nonliving Parts of an Ecosystem

The nonliving parts of an ecosystem are just as important as the living parts. The main nonliving parts of an ecosystem include sunlight, soil, air, water, and temperature. These nonliving parts interact with one another. For example, water sometimes moves soil from place to place.

The nonliving parts also interact with the living parts of the ecosystem. Salt water is a nonliving part of a mangrove swamp ecosystem. Only certain plants can live in salt water. Because of this, salt affects the ecosystem.

✔ **What are the main nonliving parts of an ecosystem?**

▲ Tall grasses and wildflowers grow in the sunlit mountain meadow. Small plants and saplings grow at the forest edge. Only a few plants grow among the trees in the forest.

Grasses and bushes can grow along the stream where there is water and plenty of light. Pine trees grow where the soil is drier. Few other plants grow in the shade under the trees. ▼

Summary

An ecosystem is made up of groups of living things and their environment. An ecosystem may include plants and animals, and nonliving parts such as sunlight, soil, air, water, and temperature. Organisms of the same species form populations. A community is made up of populations of different species in an ecosystem.

Review

1. Why do some ecosystems include many living things?
2. Is a row of bean plants in a garden a population or a community? Explain.
3. What nonliving part of the mangrove swamp limits the kinds of plants that can live there?
4. **Critical Thinking** Contrast a population with a community.
5. **Test Prep** What might an ecosystem that has mostly pine or spruce trees be called?
   A mountain forest
   B evergreen forest

LINKS

MATH LINK

www.harcourtschool.com

B16

B17

Summarize what you have read.

- Think about what you've already learned about systems and interactions.
- Ask yourself: What kind of system is an ecosystem? What interactions occur in an ecosystem?

Study the photographs and illustrations.

- Read the captions and any labels.
- Think: What kind of ecosystem is shown in the photographs? What are the nonliving parts of the ecosystem? What living parts of the ecosystem are shown?

For more reading strategies and tips, see pages R38–R49.

Reading about science helps you understand the conclusions you have made based on your investigations.

Writing to Communicate

Writing about what you are learning helps you connect the new ideas to what you already know. Scientists **write** about what they learn in their research and investigations to help others understand the work they have done. As you work like a scientist, you will use the following kinds of writing to describe what you are doing and learning.

In **informative writing,** you may

• describe your observations, inferences, and conclusions.

• tell how to do an experiment.

In **narrative writing,** you may

• describe something, give examples, or tell a story.

In **expressive writing,** you may

• write letters, poems, or songs.

In **persuasive writing,** you may

• write letters about important issues in science.

• write essays expressing your opinions about science issues.

Writing about what you have learned about science helps others understand your thinking.

Using Numbers

Scientists **use numbers** when they collect and display their data. Understanding numbers and using them to show the results of investigations are important skills that a scientist must have. As you work like a scientist, you will use numbers in the following ways:

Measuring

Scientists make accurate measurements as they gather data. They use many different measuring instruments, such as thermometers, clocks and timers, rulers, a spring scale, and a balance, and they use beakers and other containers to measure liquids.

For more information about using measuring tools, see pages R2–R6.

Interpreting Data

Scientists collect, organize, display, and interpret data as they do investigations. Scientists choose a way to display data that helps others understand what they have learned. Tables, charts, and graphs are good ways to display data so that it can be interpreted by others.

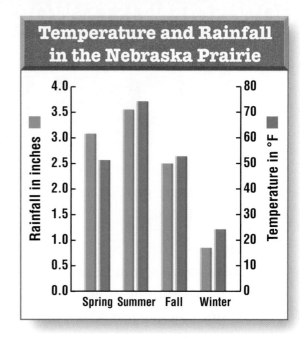

Temperature and Rainfall in the Nebraska Prairie

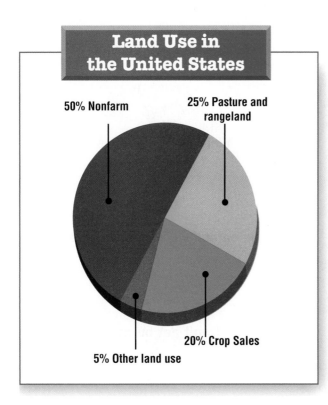

Land Use in the United States

50% Nonfarm

25% Pasture and rangeland

20% Crop Sales

5% Other land use

Using Number Sense

Scientists must understand what the numbers they use represent. They compare and order numbers, compute with numbers, read and understand the numbers shown on graphs, and read the scales on thermometers, measuring cups, beakers, and other tools.

Good scientists apply their math skills to help them display and interpret the data they collect.

In Harcourt Science you will have many opportunities to work like a scientist. An exciting year of discovery lies ahead!

Safety in Science

Doing investigations in science can be fun, but you need to be sure you do them safely. Here are some rules to follow.

1 Think ahead. Study the steps of the investigation so you know what to expect. If you have any questions, ask your teacher. Be sure you understand any safety symbols that are shown.

2 Be neat. Keep your work area clean. If you have long hair, pull it back so it doesn't get in the way. Roll or push up long sleeves to keep them away from your experiment.

3 Oops! If you should spill or break something or get cut, tell your teacher right away.

4 Watch your eyes. Wear safety goggles anytime you are directed to do so. If you get anything in your eyes, tell your teacher right away.

5 Yuck! Never eat or drink anything during a science activity unless you are told to do so by your teacher.

6 Don't get shocked. Be especially careful if an electric appliance is used. Be sure that electric cords are in a safe place where you can't trip over them. Don't ever pull a plug out of an outlet by pulling on the cord.

7 Keep it clean. Always clean up when you have finished. Put everything away and wipe your work area. Wash your hands.

In some activities you will see these symbols. They are signs for what you need to act safely.

Be especially careful.

Wear safety goggles.

Be careful with sharp objects.

Don't get burned.

Protect your clothes.

Protect your hands with mitts.

Be careful with electricity.

Forces and Motion

CHAPTER 1   **Electricity and Magnetism** **F2**

CHAPTER 2   **Motion—Forces at Work** **F36**

CHAPTER 3   **Simple Machines** **F66**

Unit Expeditions **F96**

UNIT EXPERIMENT

Strength of Electromagnets

Forces enable you to affect the world around you. You push and pull to walk, eat, and do homework. When you use appliances, you are using electric and magnetic forces. While you study this unit, you can conduct a long-term experiment about a type of magnet and its force. Here are some questions to think about. What affects the strength of an electromagnet? How does a different wire or battery size affect the magnet? Plan and conduct an experiment to find answers to these or other questions you have about forces and motion. See pages x–xix for help in designing your experiment.

1

Electricity and Magnetism

Vocabulary Preview

charge
static electricity
electric field
electric current
circuit
electric cell
conductor
insulator
resistor
series circuit
parallel circuit
magnet
magnetic pole
magnetic field
electromagnet

Snap! Crackle! Pop! Your socks crackle and spark when you separate them from your freshly dried sweater! This kind of electricity is called static electricity. You can become charged with static electricity just by dragging your feet when you walk across carpet. Then ZAP! you'll get a "charge" out of opening the next door you come to!

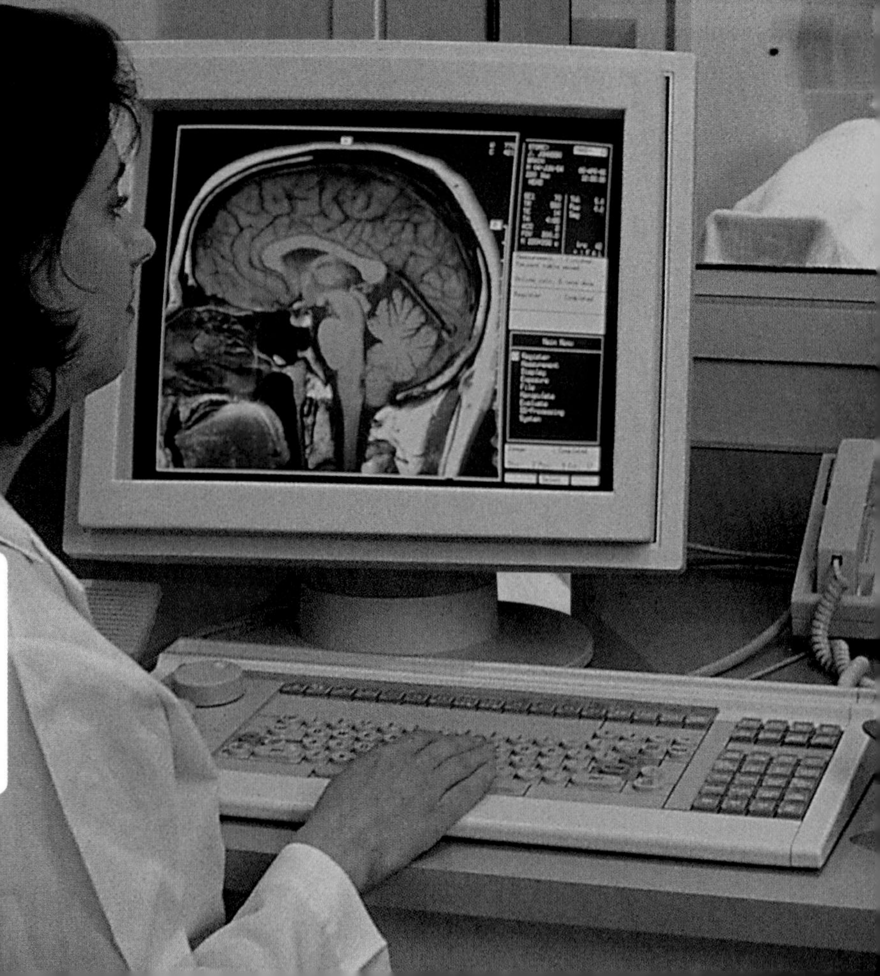

Fast Fact

MRI machines use powerful magnets to take pictures of the inside of the human body. The magnets are so strong that doctors, nurses, and patients can't carry any metal into the room where the machine is working.

Photocopiers make images by using static electricity! A large charged drum inside a photocopier pulls powdered ink to it. The ink goes to wherever dark spots on the original are reflected on the drum. The powder pattern is put on a piece of paper. Then the paper is heated and the ink melts, making a permanent copy.

Electricity use is measured in kilowatt-hours. Every home has a meter that measures how many kilowatt-hours have been used. A 60-watt light bulb uses 0.06 kilowatt-hours in one hour. Here's a list of the number of kilowatt-hours different appliances use in an hour:

Electricity Use

Appliance	Kilowatt-Hours Used in One Hour
Color television	0.23
Toaster	1.2
Hair dryer	1.5
Microwave oven	1.5
Clothes dryer	4.0
Refrigerator/freezer	5.0–7.0

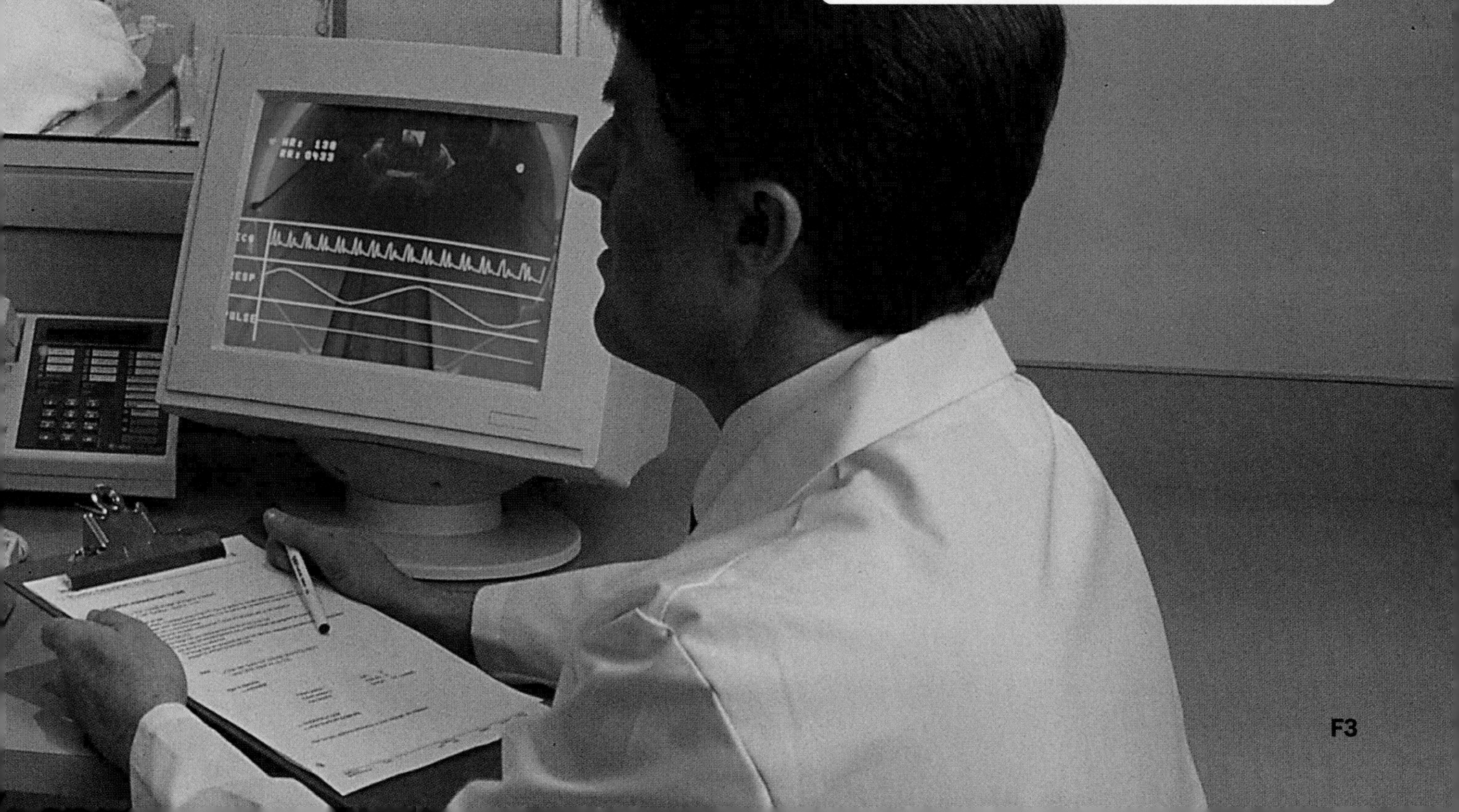

What Is Static Electricity?

In this lesson, you can . . .

INVESTIGATE rubbing balloons with different materials.

LEARN ABOUT causes of static electricity.

LINK to math, writing, health, and technology.

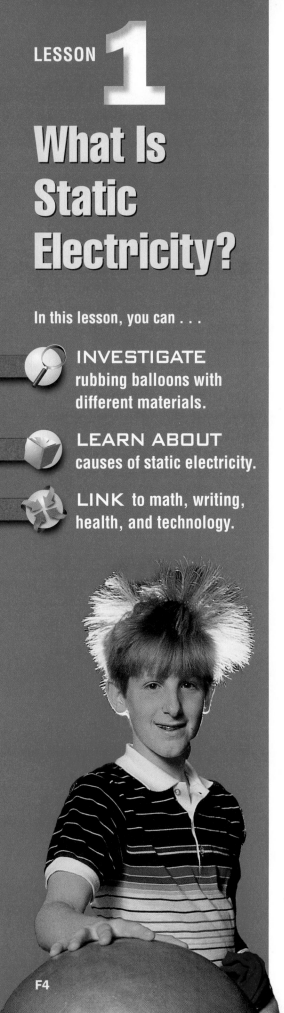

◀ It's not the wind that's making this boy's hair stand on end. It's static electricity. You may be surprised to learn what else static electricity can do.

INVESTIGATE

Balloons Rubbed with Different Materials

Activity Purpose Have you ever opened a package that had something breakable inside? There may have been little foam pieces in the box, and you may have noticed the strange way they acted. They jumped away from each other but stuck to almost everything else. You can make balloons act this way, too. In this investigation you will rub balloons with different materials. Then you'll **compare** your **observations** to **infer** why the balloons behaved the way they did.

Materials

- two small, round balloons
- string
- tape
- scrap of silk cloth
- scrap of wool cloth
- paper towel
- plastic wrap

Activity Procedure

1. Blow up the balloons, and tie them closed. Use string and tape to hang one balloon from a shelf or table.

2. Rub the silk all over each balloon. Slowly bring the free balloon near the hanging balloon. **Observe** the hanging balloon. **Record** your observations. (Picture A)

Picture A

Picture B

3. Again rub the silk all over the hanging balloon. Move the silk away. Then slowly bring the silk close to the balloon. **Observe** the hanging balloon, and **record** your observations. (Picture B)

4. Repeat Steps 2 and 3 separately with the wool, a paper towel, and plastic wrap. **Record** your **observations.**

5. Rub the silk all over the hanging balloon. Rub the wool all over the free balloon. Slowly bring the free balloon near the hanging balloon. **Observe** the hanging balloon. **Record** your observations.

Draw Conclusions

1. **Compare** your observations of the two balloons in Step 2 with your observations of a balloon and the material it was rubbed with in Steps 3 and 4.

2. **Compare** your observations of the hanging balloon in Step 2 with your observations of it in Step 5.

3. **Scientists at Work** Which of your observations support the **inference** that a force acted on the balloons and materials? Explain your answer.

Investigate Further When you rubbed the balloons, you caused a charge to build up. Like charges repel. Opposite charges attract. Review your results for each trial. Tell whether the balloons or material had like charges or opposite charges.

Process Skill Tip

A force is a push or a pull. You can **infer** a force between two objects by observing whether the objects are pulled toward each other or pushed away from each other.

Static Electricity

Two Kinds of Charge

Remember that matter is made of particles that have mass and volume. Particles of matter also have a property called *electric charge*. A particle can have a positive (+) charge, a negative (−) charge, or no charge at all.

Matter in an object normally has equal numbers of positive and negative particles. It is *neutral*. Rubbing two objects together, however, can move negative particles from one object to the other. That is exactly what happened in the Investigation. The result was that the number of positive charges on each balloon was different from the number of negative charges. **Charge** is a measure of the extra positive or negative particles that an object has. Rubbing gave one object an overall *positive charge*, and it gave the other an overall *negative charge*.

The charge that stays on an object is called **static electricity** (STAT•ik ee•lek•TRIS•ih•tee). *Static* means "not moving." Even though the charges moved to get to the object, once there they stayed.

✓ **What are the two types of charges?**

FIND OUT

- **about a property of matter called charge**
- **how charges move from one piece of matter to another**
- **how electric fields cause forces**

VOCABULARY

charge
static electricity
electric field

Positive Charge

▲ A single positive charge is labeled +. A single negative charge is labeled −. When an object has more positive charges than negative charges, its overall charge is positive.

Negative Charge

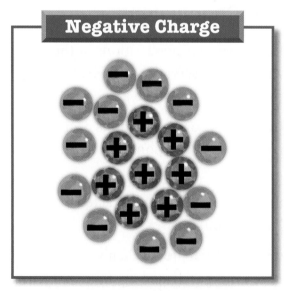

▲ If an object has more negative charges than positive charges, its overall charge is negative. How many extra negative charges are shown here?

Separating Charges

Most of the time, you, a balloon, and a doorknob have neither an overall negative charge nor an overall positive charge. You and the objects are neutral. To see the effects of forces between charges, you must separate negative charges from positive charges.

You can separate the negative and positive charges of many objects by rubbing them together. Rubbing pulls negative charges off one object onto the other. Note that only negative charges move in this way.

When you comb dry hair, the teeth of the comb rub negative charges from the hair. The comb gets extra negative charges, so it has an overall negative charge. Your hair loses negative charges. It now has an overall positive charge.

✔ **Which kind of charge moves to make a static charge?**

As clothes tumble in a dryer, different fabrics rub against each other. Negative charges move from one piece of clothing to another. When this happens the clothes stick together. ▼

▲ If you hold a piece of wool next to a balloon, nothing happens. So you know that neither the wool nor the balloon is charged. The numbers of positive and negative charges on the balloon are equal. The charges are also equal on the wool. Both items have a neutral charge.

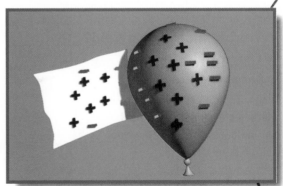

▲ Rubbing wool on a balloon separates charges. Negative charges move from the wool to the balloon. The balloon now has more negative charges than positive charges. The balloon is negatively charged. The wool loses negative charges. Now it has more positive charges than negative charges. It is positively charged.

Electric Forces

In the investigation you saw how a charged balloon pushed or pulled another charged balloon. The push or pull between objects with different charges is an *electric force.* An electric force causes two objects with opposite charges to *attract,* or pull, each other. An electric force causes two objects with like charges to *repel* (rih•PEL), or push away from, each other.

The space where electric forces occur around an object is called an **electric field**. The electric field of a positive charge attracts a nearby negative charge. The electric field of a positive charge repels a nearby positive charge.

In diagrams, arrows are used to show an electric field. They point the way one positive charge would be pulled by the field. The pictures here show the electric fields of two pairs of balloons. One pair has opposite charges. The other pair has the same charges.

✔ **What is an electric field?**

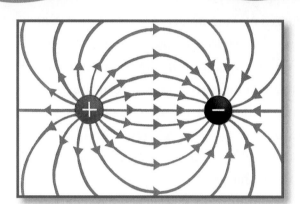

▲ One balloon has a positive charge. The other has a negative charge. Their electric fields form a closed pattern of field lines. Balloons with opposite charges attract each other.

Both balloons have negative charges. Their electric fields do not form a closed pattern of field lines. Balloons with the same type of charge repel each other.

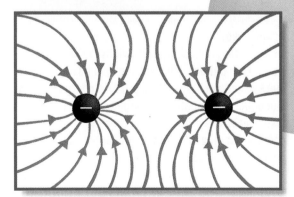

F8

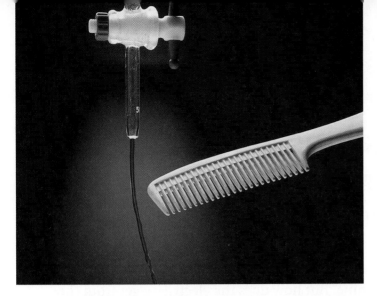

▲ After you comb your hair, your comb has a negative charge. Its electric field repels the negative particles in the stream of water. Negative particles are pushed to the opposite side of the stream. That leaves extra positive charges on the side near the comb. The stream bends toward the comb.

Summary

Objects become electrically charged when they gain or lose negative charges. A charge causes an electric field. The electric fields of charged objects interact to produce electric forces. Objects with like charges repel each other. Objects with unlike charges attract each other.

Review

1. What is static electricity?
2. What is charge?
3. What is an electric field?
4. **Critical Thinking** How can you make a piece of rubber that has an overall positive charge neutral again?
5. **Test Prep** A plastic ruler can get a positive charge by —
   A gaining a single negative charge
   B losing a single negative charge
   C gaining a single positive charge
   D losing a single positive charge

LINKS

MATH LINK

Use Addition Properties The two pictures on page F6 show charges. How many single negative charges must each object gain or lose to become neutral? Use numbers and math symbols to show how you found your answer.

WRITING LINK

Informative Writing—Description Suppose you are a balloon. Write a paragraph for a classmate describing what happens to you as you gain a negative charge from a piece of wool.

HEALTH LINK

Lightning Safety Lightning is a big movement of charged particles. It can kill people and animals, and it can start fires. Find out the safety rules you should follow during a thunderstorm. Make a poster illustrating the rules.

TECHNOLOGY LINK

Learn more about early use of electricity by visiting the National Museum of American History Internet site.
www.si.edu/harcourt/science

 Smithsonian Institution®

What Is an Electric Current?

In this lesson, you can . . .

INVESTIGATE using a battery to light a bulb.

LEARN ABOUT electric current.

LINK to math, writing, health, and technology.

INVESTIGATE

Making a Bulb Light Up

Activity Purpose Can a flashlight work without batteries? You would be right if you said *no*. The batteries produce the electricity that makes the bulb shine. But how does the electricity get from the batteries to the bulb? You can **plan and conduct a simple investigation** to find out how materials need to be arranged to make a bulb light.

Materials
- D-cell battery
- insulated electrical wire
- miniature light bulb
- masking tape

Activity Procedure

1 Make a chart like the one shown on the next page. You will use it to **record** your **observations**.

2 **Predict** a way to arrange the materials you have been given so that the bulb lights up. Make a drawing to **record** your prediction. (Picture A)

3 Test your prediction. **Record** whether or not the bulb lights up. (Picture B)

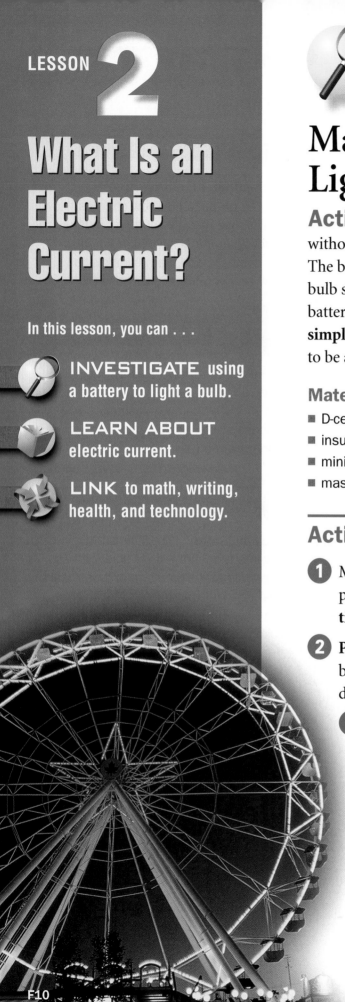

◀ The lights of a Ferris wheel shine in the night as the wheel goes round and round. The electricity that makes the bulbs glow and moves the wheel also goes round and round.

Picture A

Picture B

Predictions and Observations

Arrangement of Bulb, Battery, and Wire	Drawing	Observations

4 Continue to work with the bulb, the battery, and the wire. Try different arrangements to get the bulb to light. **Record** the results of each try.

Draw Conclusions

1. What did you **observe** about the arrangement of materials when the bulb lighted?

2. What did you **observe** about the arrangement of materials when the bulb did NOT light?

3. **Scientists at Work** To find out more about bulbs and batteries, you could **plan an investigation** of your own. To do that, you need to decide the following: What question do you want to answer? What materials will you need? How will you use the materials? What will you observe?

Investigate Further **Conduct your investigation.**

Process Skill Tip

When you **plan and conduct a simple investigation**, you work to find the answer to a question or to solve a problem. By doing many tests and observing their outcomes, you can draw conclusions about how something works.

F11

Electric Currents

Moving Charges

You know that a static charge stays on an object. But even a static charge will move if it has a path to follow. The snap and crackle of a static electric shock are the result of a moving charge.

Have you ever gotten a small electric shock from touching a doorknob? Here's how it happens. Walking on a carpet rubs negative charges off the carpet and onto your feet. The charges spread out on your body. Your whole body becomes negatively charged. When you touch the doorknob, all the extra negative charges move at once from your hand to the doorknob. You get a small "zap." The static, or unmoving charge, has become a *current*, or moving charge. A flow of electric charges is called an **electric current**. Current is measured in amperes (AM•peers).

In the investigation you arranged a wire, a bulb, and a battery to make a path in which negative charges could flow. A path that is made for an electric current is called a **circuit** (SER•kit). The battery was an important part of the circuit you made. A battery is an **electric cell**, which supplies energy to move charges through a circuit. The energy a battery can provide is measured in volts.

✔ **What does an electric current need in order to flow?**

FIND OUT

- how electric charges can move
- ways different materials control electric current
- differences between series and parallel circuits

VOCABULARY

electric current
circuit
electric cell
conductor
insulator
resistor
series circuit
parallel circuit

◀ An electric current in a circuit moves like a bike wheel. When you pedal, you give energy of motion to the whole wheel at once. When you connect a circuit, a battery moves energy to all parts of the circuit at the same time.

◀ Use your finger to trace the path of the current through each part of the circuit. What do you notice?

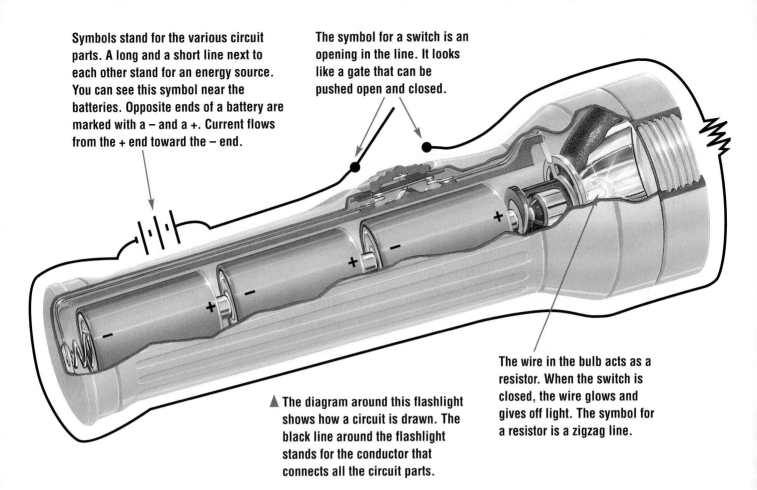

Symbols stand for the various circuit parts. A long and a short line next to each other stand for an energy source. You can see this symbol near the batteries. Opposite ends of a battery are marked with a – and a +. Current flows from the + end toward the – end.

The symbol for a switch is an opening in the line. It looks like a gate that can be pushed open and closed.

The wire in the bulb acts as a resistor. When the switch is closed, the wire glows and gives off light. The symbol for a resistor is a zigzag line.

▲ The diagram around this flashlight shows how a circuit is drawn. The black line around the flashlight stands for the conductor that connects all the circuit parts.

Controlling Current

A circuit with a battery, bulb, and wires contains different materials such as copper and plastic. You can classify these materials by the way they control the flow of charges through them.

A **conductor** is a material that current can pass through easily. Most metals are good conductors of electric current. Electric wires are made of metal, often copper. The base of a light bulb is made of metal because it must conduct an electric current.

A material that current cannot pass through easily is called an **insulator** (IN•suh•layt•er). The black band between the metal tip and the screw-in part of a light bulb is an insulator. A plastic covering insulated the wire you used in the investigation. Plastic keeps the metal of the wire from touching other metal.

A flashlight has a switch to turn it on and off. A *switch* uses conductors and insulators to make and break a circuit. When the switch is on, two conductors touch. When they touch, the path is complete. Current flows through the circuit. When the switch is off, air separates the two conductors, breaking the path. No current can flow.

Some materials cut down, or resist, the flow of charges. A material that resists but doesn't stop the flow of current is called a **resistor** (rih•ZIS•ter). A flashlight bulb contains a tiny coil of metal. The coil is a resistor. As charges move through the resistor, they transfer thermal energy to it. The metal becomes hot. The glowing coil transfers some of its thermal energy to the air as radiation. It gives off light.

✔ **What does a switch do in a circuit?**

Series Circuits

When you turn on a flashlight, there is one path for the current to follow through the circuit. A circuit that has only one path for the current is called a **series circuit**. The pictures below show a series circuit with two bulbs. Note that the current runs from the battery to one bulb, then to the next bulb, and then back to the battery. What happens if you remove one bulb or a bulb burns out? The single path is broken. No current moves through the circuit. As a result, the second bulb will go out.

✔ **How does current travel in a series circuit?**

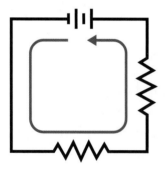

▲ As the arrow shows, there is only one path for current in a series circuit. Disconnecting a light bulb opens the whole circuit, so both bulbs go out.

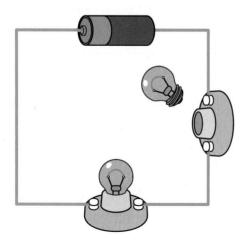

Parallel Circuits

A **parallel** (PAIR•uh•lel) **circuit** has more than one path for current to travel. With your finger, trace the path of the current in the parallel circuit shown below. Part of the current moves through each path of the circuit. What happens when a bulb is removed from this circuit? The current still moves through the other path. The second bulb stays lit. If one bulb in a parallel circuit burns out, the other bulbs will stay on.

✔ **Which type of circuit has more than one path for current?**

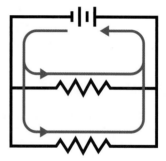

▲ Notice how the arrow splits in two. There are at least two paths for current in a parallel circuit. Disconnecting a bulb opens only one path. The other bulb stays lit.

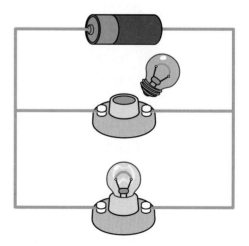

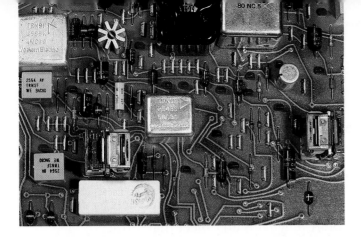

▲ Circuits inside appliances are a mix of many parallel and series circuits.

Summary

Electric current is a flow of charges through a path called a circuit. A material in a circuit can be classified as a conductor, an insulator, or a resistor. If a circuit has one path for current, it is a series circuit. A parallel circuit has more than one path for current.

Review

1. What is an electric current?
2. Describe what has to be in place for a circuit to work.
3. Contrast conductors and insulators.
4. **Critical Thinking** Most wall outlets in your home have places for two plugs. Infer which type of circuit an outlet is part of. How do you know?
5. **Test Prep** What supplies energy in an electric circuit?
   A conductors
   B electric cells
   C resistors
   D switches

 LINKS

 MATH LINK

Solve a Problem Electric energy is measured in a unit called a kilowatt-hour, or kWh. With a parent's permission, read the electric meter at your home twice, one week apart. Use the readings to calculate how many kWh were used. If each kWh costs 10 cents, how much did a week of electricity use cost?

 WRITING LINK

Descriptive Writing—Personal Story In the United States, electricity is a part of almost everyone's life. Suppose you woke up one morning and electricity no longer worked anywhere. Write a story describing what a day completely without electricity would be like.

 HEALTH LINK

Electricity Safety The batteries you have been using are safe because they are low voltage. Higher voltage household current can hurt people or start fires. Use library resources to find out more about home electricity safety. Then share what you learned with your family and conduct an electricity safety survey of your home.

 TECHNOLOGY LINK

Learn more about controlling large circuits by viewing *L.A. Traffic Control* on the **Harcourt Science Newsroom Video.**

What Is a Magnet?

In this lesson, you can . . .

 INVESTIGATE how a compass works.

 LEARN ABOUT the ways magnets interact.

 LINK to math, writing, social studies, and technology.

INVESTIGATE

A Compass

Activity Purpose If you are like most people, you have papers stuck with magnets to your refrigerator. A *magnet* is an object that attracts certain materials, mainly iron and steel. The material in your refrigerator magnet attracts the steel in your refrigerator door. The attraction is strong enough that it works through paper. In this investigation you will make your own magnet and, based on your **observations, infer** how a compass works.

Materials

- safety goggles
- small bar magnet
- small objects made of iron or steel, such as paper clips
- large sewing needle or straight pin (4–5 cm long)
- small piece of foam tray
- cup of water

Activity Procedure — CAUTION

1. **CAUTION** **Put on your safety goggles.** Hold the bar magnet near a paper clip. **Observe** what happens. Now hold the needle near the paper clip. Observe what happens.

2. **CAUTION** **Be careful with sharp objects.** Hold the needle by its eye and drag its entire length over the magnet 20 times, always in the same direction. (Picture A)

◄ The compass is an important tool that helps sailors find their way across the oceans.

Picture A

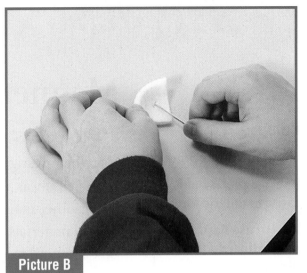

Picture B

3 Repeat Step 1. **Observe** what happens.

4 Hold the foam on a flat surface. From one side, slide the needle into the foam with the point away from your fingers. **CAUTION** **Be careful with sharp objects.** (Picture B)

5 Move the bar magnet at least a meter from the cup. Float the foam in the water. **Observe** what happens to the needle.

6 Carefully and slowly turn the cup. **Observe** what happens to the needle.

7 Hold one end of the bar magnet near the cup. **Observe** what happens to the needle. Switch magnet ends. What happens?

Draw Conclusions

1. Describe what happened when you floated the foam with the needle in water. What happened when you turned the cup?

2. What happened when you brought the bar magnet near the floating needle?

3. **Scientists at Work** What **hypothesis** can you make based on your observations of the needle? What predictions can you make by using your hypothesis?

Investigate Further **Plan and conduct an experiment** to test your hypothesis from Question 3, above.

Process Skill Tip

When you **hypothesize**, you carefully explain all your observations. A hypothesis is more detailed than an inference. Unlike an inference, a hypothesis can be used to make predictions that you can test.

Magnets

Two Poles

FIND OUT

- about magnetic poles
- how magnetic fields cause magnetic forces
- how to use Earth's magnetic field to find directions

VOCABULARY

magnet
magnetic pole
magnetic field

In the investigation you made a needle into a magnet. You could tell it was a magnet because it attracted metal paper clips, just as other magnets do. A **magnet** is an object that attracts certain materials, usually objects made of iron or steel. A needle isn't a natural magnet. You changed it into a magnet by dragging it along the bar magnet.

A magnet has two ends called **magnetic poles**, or just *poles* for short. A magnet's pull is strongest at the poles. If a bar magnet can swing freely, one end, called the *north-seeking pole*, will always point north. The opposite end, called the *south-seeking pole*, will always point south. A magnet's north-seeking pole is usually marked *N*. Its south-seeking pole is marked *S*.

✔ **What is each end of a magnet called?**

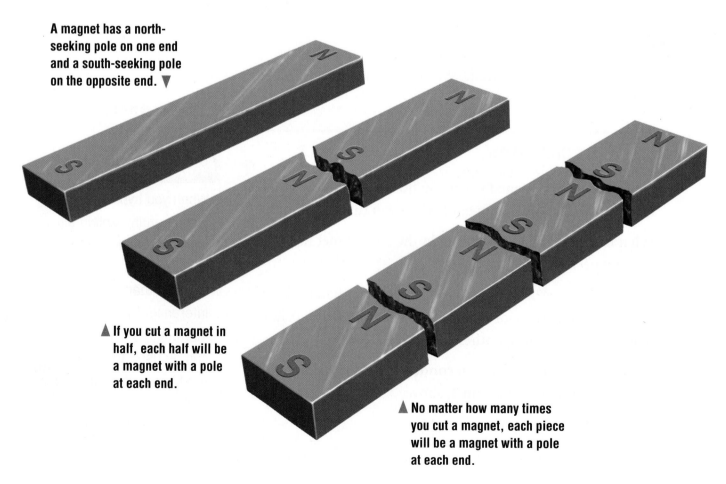

A magnet has a north-seeking pole on one end and a south-seeking pole on the opposite end. ▼

▲ If you cut a magnet in half, each half will be a magnet with a pole at each end.

▲ No matter how many times you cut a magnet, each piece will be a magnet with a pole at each end.

Magnetic Forces

If you've ever played with magnets, you've probably felt them pull toward each other. At other times they seem to push away from each other. The forces you felt are magnetic forces caused by magnetic fields.

A **magnetic field** is the space all around a magnet where the force of the magnet can act. You can't see the field. However, a magnet can move iron filings into lines. The pattern made by the iron filings shows the shape of the magnet's field.

Forces between magnet poles are like forces between electric charges. Opposite magnetic poles attract, and like poles repel. If the N pole of one magnet is held toward the S pole of another magnet, their fields form a closed pattern. This closed pattern of lines shows a force that pulls the magnets together.

If two magnets are held with their N poles near each other, their magnetic fields form an open pattern of lines. Just as with electric charges, this pattern shows a force that pushes the magnets away from each other.

✔ **Where is the pull of a magnet strongest?**

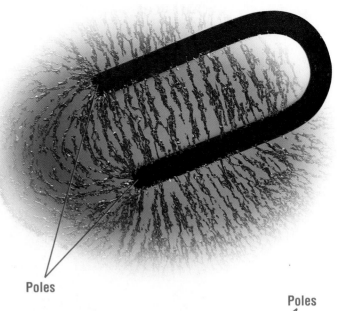

Poles

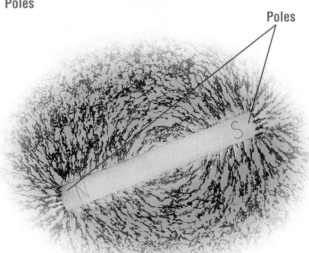

Poles

▲ The shape of a magnetic field depends on the shape of the magnet. The bunching of iron filings on the end of a magnet shows that the magnetic force is strongest at a magnet's poles.

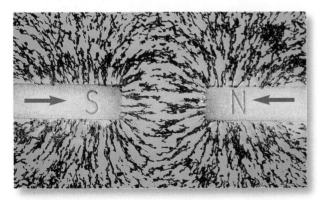

▲ Opposite poles of two magnets attract. The pattern of iron filings is closed. This shows a magnetic force that attracts, or pulls, the magnets together.

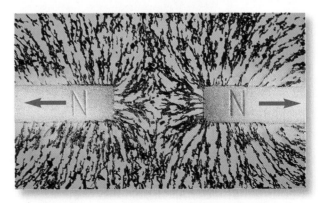

▲ Like poles of two magnets repel. The field lines are open, showing lines of force that push the magnets apart.

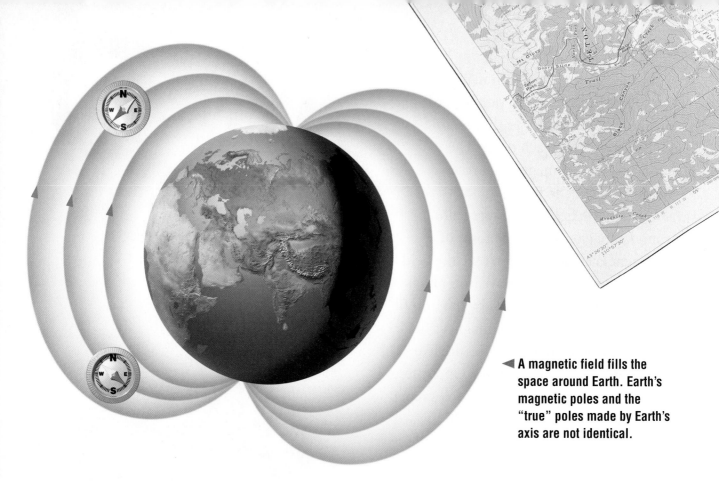

◀ A magnetic field fills the space around Earth. Earth's magnetic poles and the "true" poles made by Earth's axis are not identical.

Compasses

The north-seeking and south-seeking property of magnets is useful. For hundreds of years, people have used magnets to find direction. The first magnets used were made of a heavy natural material called *lodestone*. Today geologists know this material as the mineral magnetite.

A compass today uses a lightweight magnetic needle that is free to turn. This is much like the needle you made into a magnet in the investigation. A compass needle points along an imaginary line connecting the North and South Poles. This is because Earth is like a giant magnet.

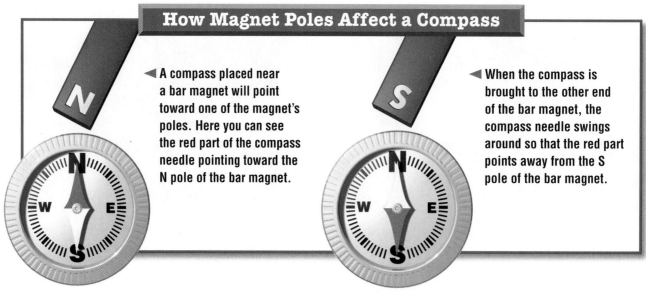

How Magnet Poles Affect a Compass

◀ A compass placed near a bar magnet will point toward one of the magnet's poles. Here you can see the red part of the compass needle pointing toward the N pole of the bar magnet.

◀ When the compass is brought to the other end of the bar magnet, the compass needle swings around so that the red part points away from the S pole of the bar magnet.

LINKS

MATH LINK

Make a Bar Graph Decide on a way to measure the strength of different bar magnets or different magnet shapes. Test some magnets. Then use a computer program such as *Graph Links* to make a bar graph to show what you measured.

◄ When there are no landmarks you know, a map and a compass can help you find your way.

The field lines of Earth's magnetic field come together close to the planet's North and South Poles. This pattern is like the one shown by the iron filings around the bar magnet on page F19. Indeed, Earth's magnetic field is like the field of a giant bar magnet.

WRITING LINK

Informative Writing—How-to Write a paragraph telling a classmate how to use a compass to find the direction in which he or she is traveling.

✔ **How does a compass work?**

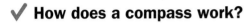

Summary

Magnets are objects that attract materials such as iron. Every magnet has two magnetic poles. Magnetic forces are caused by the interaction of magnetic fields. Earth's magnetic field is like the field of a bar magnet. A compass needle interacts with Earth's magnetic field.

SOCIAL STUDIES LINK

Earth's Moving Magnetic Poles Earth's north magnetic pole is constantly moving. Find out how the pole's location is shown on topographical (tahp•uh•GRAF•ih•kuhl) maps, which show the land's surface features, and on navigational charts. Find the current location of the north magnetic pole on a globe. Measure the distance between the true North Pole and the magnetic north pole.

Review

1. How can you find the poles of a magnet?

2. What is a magnetic field?

3. Which type of magnet has a field that is about the same shape as the magnetic field of Earth?

4. **Critical Thinking** Describe the field lines formed if the south poles of two magnets are brought close together.

5. **Test Prep** How many poles does a magnet have?

   A none

   B one

   C two

   D four

 TECHNOLOGY LINK

ONLINE

Learn more about Earth's magnetic field by visiting the National Air and Space Museum Internet site.
www.si.edu/harcourt/science

 Smithsonian Institution®

LESSON 4

What Is an Electro-magnet?

In this lesson, you can . . .

INVESTIGATE the magnetic field around a wire that carries current.

LEARN ABOUT uses of electromagnets.

LINK to math, writing, language arts, and technology.

Strong magnetic forces lift this train slightly from the tracks and push it forward. ▽

INVESTIGATE

How Magnets and Electricity Can Interact

Activity Purpose The pictures at the bottom of page F20 show how a bar magnet affects a nearby compass. Have you ever tried this yourself? In this investigation you will **observe** how a bar magnet affects a compass needle. You'll **compare** it with the way a current in a wire affects a compass needle. You can then **infer** some things about electricity moving through wires.

Materials

- bar magnet
- small compass
- sheet of cardboard
- tape
- insulated wire, about 30 cm long, with stripped ends
- D-cell battery

Activity Procedure

1 Try several positions of the magnet and compass. **Record** your **observations** of how the magnet affects the compass needle.

2 Place the compass flat on the cardboard so the needle is lined up with north. Tape the middle third of the insulated wire onto the cardboard in a north-south line.

3 Tape one end of the wire to the flat end of a D-cell battery. Tape the battery to the cardboard. (Picture A)

4 Without moving the cardboard, put the compass on the taped-down part of the wire.

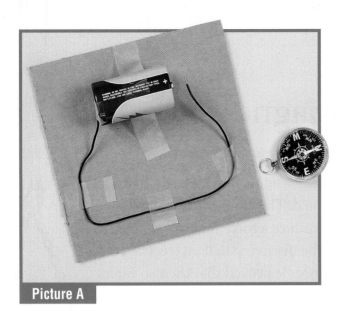

Picture A

Picture B

5 Touch the free end of the wire to the (+) end of the battery for a second. (Picture B) **Observe** the compass needle. Repeat this step several more times. **Record** your observations.

6 Carefully remove a piece of tape. Place the compass underneath the wire so that both line up along a north-south line. **Predict** what will happen if you repeat Step 5.

7 Repeat Step 5. **Record** your observations.

Draw Conclusions

1. **Compare** your observations in Step 5 with those in Step 7. Was your prediction accurate? Explain.

2. Using what you know about compasses in magnetic fields, what can you **infer** about currents in wires?

3. **Scientists at Work** Just as you predicted what would happen in Step 7, scientists often **predict** the outcome of an experiment based on their observations and inferences. Based on your observations, what would you predict will happen in this experiment if the current is made to move in the opposite direction?

Investigate Further Test your **prediction**. Remove the battery from the cardboard. Turn it so that its ends are pointing in the opposite direction. Attach the wire again. **Record** your **observations**.

Process Skill Tip

When you **predict**, you tell what you expect to happen. A prediction is based on patterns of observations. If you think you know the cause of an event, you can predict when it will happen again. Predictions aren't always correct.

Electromagnets

Currents Make Magnets

- how electricity and magnetism are related
- ways to change the strength of an electromagnet
- uses of motors and generators

VOCABULARY

electromagnet

In the past, scientists wondered if electric charge and magnetism were related. They knew that charged objects and magnets both produce a force that can pull or push without touching. The discovery that an electric current can turn a compass needle proved that the two forces are related.

A current in a wire produces a magnetic field around the wire. You saw evidence of this in the investigation. The magnetic field produced by current moved the compass needle.

If you could see them, the field lines around a wire that carries current would look different from those around a bar magnet. They circle around the wire instead of looping out from the wire ends. A compass needle moves to point along magnetic field lines. So, it moves to point at right angles to the wire.

When current flows in the wire, it produces a circular magnetic field. The compass needle lines up with the field lines by turning at right angles to the wire. ▶

When the switch is open, current no longer flows and the magnetic field goes away. The compass needle swings back to its original position. ▶

F24

This coil of wire is carrying an electric current. Iron filings show the shape of the magnetic field inside the coil. The lines of filings are closest together where the field is strongest. ▶

Compared with bar magnets, current-carrying wires produce weak magnetic fields. But there's a way to put a lot of wire in one place. When a current-carrying wire is coiled, the fields of the loops overlap. The strengths of the fields add up. The more loops you put together, the stronger the field gets.

The fields produced by many wire coils add up to make a field like that of a bar magnet. Iron filings line up along the middle of the coil. Outside the coil, the magnetic field lines loop out from one open end and back to the other.

Alone, a coil of wire easily bends. To make it stiffer and easier to use, the coil is wrapped around a solid material called a

core. This arrangement of wire wrapped around a core is called an **electromagnet** (ee•LEK•troh•mag•nit). An electromagnet is a temporary magnet. There is a magnetic field only when there is an electric current in the wire.

If the core of an electromagnet is made of iron, the core also becomes a magnet when there is current in the wire. This makes the electromagnet stronger.

✔ **Why is an electromagnet a temporary magnet?**

◀ This big electromagnet on a crane can lift a heavy load of scrap metal. It has an iron core and many wire coils, and it carries a strong current. What will happen when the current to the electromagnet is turned off?

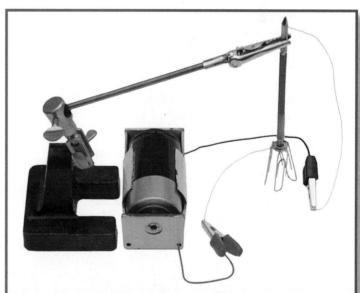
▲ When current flows through an electromagnet, the electromagnet acts like a bar magnet. This one is strong enough to hold three paper clips.

Controlling Electromagnets

A magnet and an electromagnet have one main difference. An electromagnet is a temporary magnet. You can turn it on and off with a switch. A bar magnet is a permanent magnet. It doesn't have an *off* switch. Electromagnets are a useful tool because you can control them. You can learn how one is used in The Inside Story.

Turning an electromagnet on and off is one way to control it. You can also control the strength of an electromagnet. One way to do this is to add or remove coils of wire. The more coils an electromagnet has, the stronger it is.

The amount of current also affects the strength of an electromagnet. The more current that is flowing, the stronger the electromagnet is.

Electromagnets today are made to use large amounts of current to lift large amounts of weight. Smaller and weaker ones are also made. Small electromagnets work out of sight inside computer disk drives, video players, television screens, and other electronic devices.

✔ **What is the main difference between a bar magnet and an electromagnet?**

THE INSIDE STORY

Alarm Bell

The bells used in fire alarms, doorbells, and telephones work because electromagnets can be turned off and on very quickly. The picture and diagram on the right show you how an electric bell works.

1. When the bell is turned on, current flows in the electromagnet. The electromagnet pulls the long iron rod into the coils.

2. The hammer is connected to the rod. It moves and strikes the bell, making a sound.

3. The strip of metal with the hammer acts like a switch. As the hammer moves to strike the bell, the switch opens. No current flows in the circuit. The electromagnet is turned off. The hammer returns to its original position.

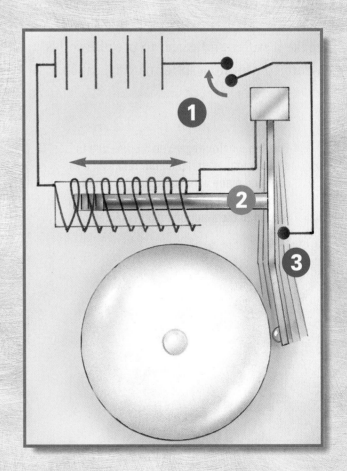

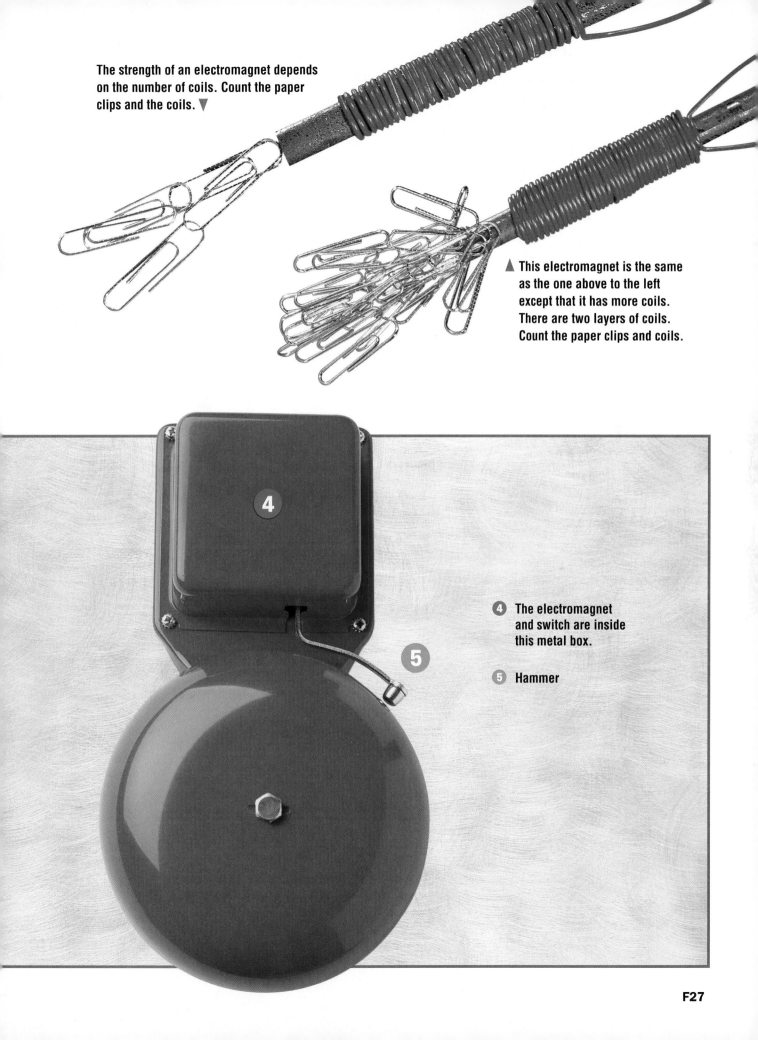

The strength of an electromagnet depends on the number of coils. Count the paper clips and the coils. ▼

▲ This electromagnet is the same as the one above to the left except that it has more coils. There are two layers of coils. Count the paper clips and coils.

4 The electromagnet and switch are inside this metal box.

5 Hammer

Motors and Generators

If electricity can produce a magnetic field, can a magnetic field produce electricity? Yes! If you move a coil of wire near a magnet, current flows in the wire. Current flows as long as the wire is moving through magnetic field lines. This is how an electric generator works.

A coil of wire, a magnet, and electricity can also be used to cause motion. That's how an electric motor works. The coil of an electromagnet is pushed and pulled by the poles of other magnets. The coil turns. This turning motion is used in machines such as kitchen appliances, toys, and tools.

✔ **What things do generators and motors have in common?**

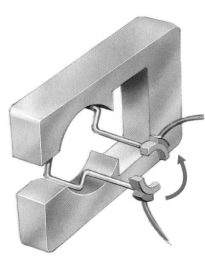

▲ One simple electric motor contains an electromagnet and a permanent magnet. When the motor is on, the direction of current is changed in a pattern. As it changes, the coil is pushed and then pulled by the permanent magnet. The coil turns.

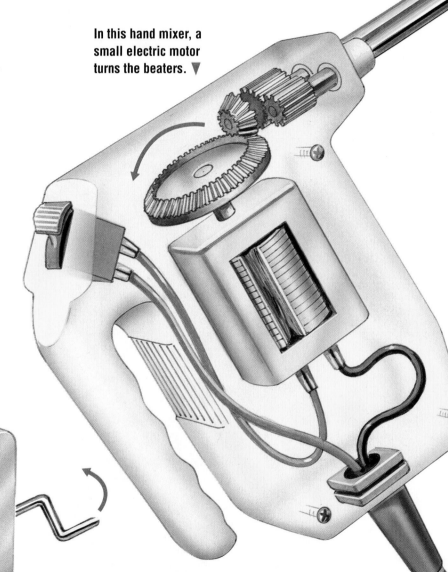

In this hand mixer, a small electric motor turns the beaters. ▼

◄ A small, simple generator uses a hand crank to turn a magnet around a loop of wire. Generators that supply electric power for homes and factories are much bigger, about the size of a bus. They usually use steam or water power to turn a coil.

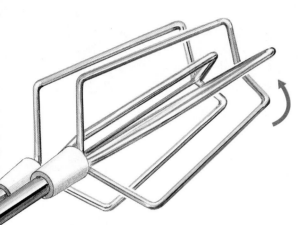

Summary

Wires carrying an electric current become magnets. An electromagnet is a core wrapped with wires that carry current. The ends of the electromagnet's coil are its poles. An electromagnet is magnetic only when there is a current in the wire. Generators use electromagnets to produce current from motion. Motors use electromagnets to produce motion from current.

Review

1. What do magnets and electric charges have in common?

2. Name two ways that you can make an electromagnet stronger.

3. What is a motor?

4. **Critical Thinking** Why is it useful to have a magnet that can be turned on and off?

5. **Test Prep** The ends of an electromagnet that are useful are called —

   A cores
   B loops
   C poles
   D wires

LINKS

MATH LINK

Find a Rule An electromagnet with 10 loops of wire can pick up 5 paper clips. With 20 loops it can pick up 10 paper clips. Predict how many paper clips the electromagnet can pick up if it has 40 loops. Write a procedure to find out how many paper clips this electromagnet can pick up if you know the number of loops of wire.

WRITING LINK

Informative Writing—Description Think of an appliance in your home that has an electric motor. Write a description for a younger child, telling what the appliance does. If there were no electric motors, how would you do what the appliance does?

LANGUAGE ARTS LINK

Making Words The word *electromagnet* was made by joining two words. What are they? Research these two words to find out where they came from and how old they are. Why do you think this word is used to describe the device you learned about in this lesson?

 GO
ONLINE **TECHNOLOGY LINK**

Visit the Harcourt Learning Site for related links, activities, and resources.
www.harcourtschool.com

WELCOME TO
THE LEARNING SITE

F29

Discovering ELECTROMAGNETISM

Have you used a computer today? Answered the telephone or the doorbell? Watched television? These are just a few examples of everyday machines that work because of electromagnetism.

The First Discoveries

The early Greeks were the first people to observe and describe static electricity. They noticed that rubbing amber, a yellowish gemstone, with a cloth caused the amber to attract bits of straw or feathers. The Greek word for amber is *elektron*. Our words *electron* and *electricity* come from this Greek word.

The Greeks were also the first to observe and describe magnetism. Thales (THAY•leez), a Greek philosopher, lived in a town called Magnesia. Some of the rocks near his town seemed to pull at the shepherds' walking sticks, which had iron tips. Thales noted that the rocks also pulled toward each other and toward all iron objects that were close to them. These rocks were magnetite, a natural magnet. Later, people in Europe called this natural magnet *lodestone* (LOHD•stohn), which means *leading stone*.

The Chinese may have been the first to use magnets as compasses. Sailors and other travelers found that lodestone always turns to point along a north-south line. Compasses could be made by putting a thin piece of lodestone on a piece of wood floating in water. Later, lodestone was used to magnetize iron compass needles.

Learning More About Electricity

In the 1700s scientists began experimenting with electricity and magnetism, which they thought might be related. One of the scientists, Alessandro Volta (ah•leh•SAHN•droh VOHL•tah), discovered that he could make electricity by using pieces of two different metals. He made the first battery, which was called a voltaic (vohl•TAY•ik) pile. Using this battery moved electricity steadily through a conductor,

The History of Electricity and Magnetism

Chinese 2300 B.C.
Chinese invent magnetic compass.

Franklin 1752
Benjamin Franklin observes a spark from a kite string.

2300 B.C.   600 B.C.

Thales 600 B.C.
Thales studies magnetism.

such as a salt solution, instead of giving off the electricity all at once, like a lightning bolt or a spark caused by static electricity.

The key to understanding the connection between electricity and magnetism came from a chance observation. While giving a demonstration for a class, Hans Oersted (HAHNZ ER•stuhd) noticed that when he put a compass over a wire carrying electricity, the compass needle moved. He went on to prove that an electric current always produces a magnetic field.

Other scientists built on Oersted's discovery. Michael Faraday invented a generator, a machine that produces electricity. The generator makes electricity from a moving magnet and a coil of wire.

James Clerk Maxwell also studied Oersted's work. Maxwell hypothesized that electric and magnetic fields work together to make radiant energy, or light. About 20

Amber and feathers

years after Maxwell's experiments, Heinrich (HYN•rik) Hertz proved Maxwell was right.

Superconductors

In 1911 Dutch scientist Heike Onnes (HY•kuh AW•nuhs) discovered super-conductors. At very low temperatures, near ¯273°C (¯459°F), these metals or mixtures of metals conduct electrical current without any resistance. Superconductors are part of MRI machines, which are used by doctors to make images of the inside of the human body. In the early 2000s, trains that float above their tracks using superconducting magnets were being built and tested in Japan.

THINK ABOUT IT

1. How did observation and curiosity help Oersted?
2. How has the research of Thales, Volta, Faraday, and others affected your life?

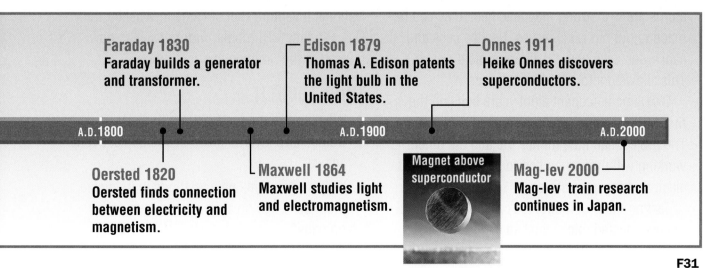

Faraday 1830
Faraday builds a generator and transformer.

Edison 1879
Thomas A. Edison patents the light bulb in the United States.

Onnes 1911
Heike Onnes discovers superconductors.

A.D.1800   A.D.1900   A.D.2000

Oersted 1820
Oersted finds connection between electricity and magnetism.

Maxwell 1864
Maxwell studies light and electromagnetism.

Magnet above superconductor

Mag-lev 2000
Mag-lev train research continues in Japan.

F31

Raymond V. Damadian
INVENTOR

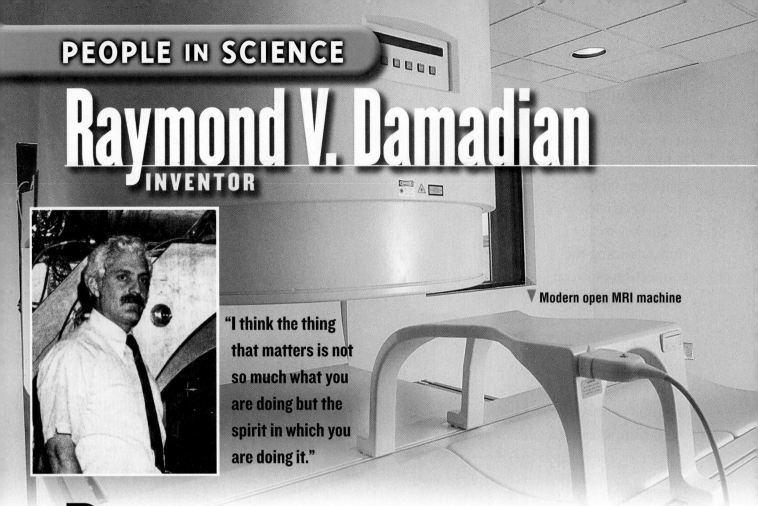

"I think the thing that matters is not so much what you are doing but the spirit in which you are doing it."

▼ Modern open MRI machine

Dr. Raymond Damadian had many interests besides science as he was growing up. He was an accomplished violinist by the time he was eight. He attended The Juilliard School of Music before becoming a doctor. He also was a professional tennis player.

Dr. Damadian and his co-workers invented the magnetic resonance imaging machine (MRI). An MRI machine uses very strong magnets to take pictures of the inside of the body. When certain atoms are in a strong magnetic field, they can be made to put out radio waves. Healthy cells and cancerous cells give off different radio waves. This allows doctors to detect cancer.

Dr. Damadian spent eight years building the first MRI machine, which he named *Indomitable*. The project had little money. He and the others working with him often had to buy equipment at electronics surplus stores.

Testing the first model took many years. First, the team tested mice who had cancer. Finally,

they tried to test it on Damadian himself, but he was too big for the machine! They found a smaller man to test the machine, and produced the first human body MRI scan in 1977.

MRI has many good qualities. It is safer than many other tests. No surgery is needed. A patient gets no dangerous radiation. MRI "sees" through bone and can produce a clearer picture than X rays.

In 1989 Damadian was inducted into the National Inventors Hall of Fame in Washington, D.C. His first MRI model, *Indomitable*, is now housed at the Smithsonian Institution.

THINK ABOUT IT

1. What sort of magnets do you think Dr. Damadian's MRI machine used? Explain your answer.

2. Why do you think new methods in medicine must be tested on animals and then on humans?

TEST CONDUCTIVITY

How can you test for conductors and insulators?

Materials

- wire, 3 pieces
- light bulb
- D-cell battery
- Test objects such as aluminum foil, coins, salt, distilled water, salt water, rubber balloon, Mylar balloon, plastic wrap, craft stick, steel wool, paper

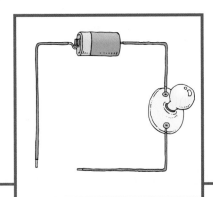

Procedure

❶ Build a series circuit like the one shown. Touch the two wire ends together to make sure your circuit works.

❷ Try to complete the circuit by touching both wires to one of the test objects. Observe the bulb carefully. Record your observations.

❸ Repeat Step 2 for each of the test objects.

❹ Try again, this time holding the wire ends farther apart when they touch each object.

Draw Conclusions

Which materials were good conductors of electricity? How do you know?

MAKE A GENERATOR

How can you use a magnet to produce a current?

Materials

- bar magnet
- tape
- cardboard
- compass
- insulated wire, 100 cm with ends stripped

Procedure

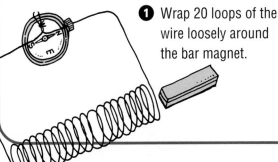

❶ Wrap 20 loops of the wire loosely around the bar magnet.

Twist the stripped ends of the wire tightly together.

❷ Tape a length of the unlooped section of wire to the cardboard. Tape the compass under the wire so the needle lines up with the wire.

❸ Move the magnet back and forth inside the loops of wire. Observe what happens to the compass needle.

Draw Conclusions

Describe how the compass needle behaves. Explain why this happened.

Vocabulary Review

Use the terms below to complete the sentences. The page numbers in ( ) tell you where to look in the chapter if you need help.

charge (F6)
static electricity (F6)
electric fields (F8)
electric current (F12)
circuit (F12)
electric cell (F12)
conductor (F13)
insulator (F13)
resistor (F13)
series circuit (F14)
parallel circuit (F14)
magnet (F18)
magnetic pole (F18)
magnetic fields (F19)
electromagnet (F25)

1. A pathway for current is called a ____.

2. ____ and ____ are similar because they are both areas where forces can act without objects touching.

3. Current passes easily through a ____ but doesn't pass easily through an ____.

4. A core wrapped in a wire that is carrying current is called an ____.

5. A measure of the extra charges that are on an object is called ____.

6. A material that resists the flow of current is called a ____.

7. An ____ is a flow of charges.

8. In a ____, taking out one light does not turn off the whole circuit.

9. The charge that stays on an object is called ____.

10. A ____ attracts objects made of iron or steel.

11. A ____ has only one path for the current.

12. Energy to move current through a circuit is supplied by an ____.

13. A ____ is where a magnet's pull is strongest.

Connect Concepts

Use the terms in the Word Bank to complete the concept map.

poles
negative
charges
attract
north
repel
positive
south

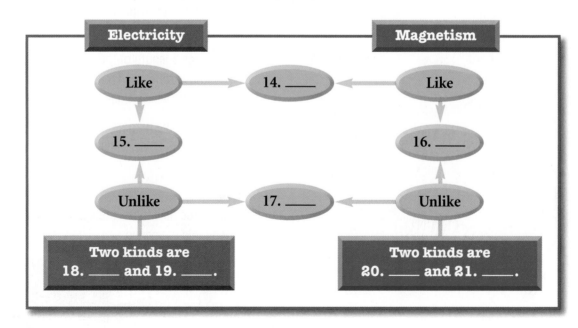

Check Understanding

Write the letter of the best choice.

22. An object has a ____ charge if it has extra positive charges.
    A large   C negative
    B neutral   D positive

23. If the electric fields of two charged objects form a closed pattern of field lines, the objects are ____ charged.
    F negatively   H neutrally
    G positively   J oppositely

24. If one bulb is removed from a series circuit, the other bulbs will —
    A dim   C flicker
    G get brighter   D go out

25. The strip of material that glows in a light bulb is —
    F a charge   H a conductor
    G an insulator   J a resistor

26. A device that produces motion energy from electrical energy is —
    A a compass   C an electromagnet
    B a generator   D a motor

Critical Thinking

27. Look at the circuit below. What will happen to each bulb if Switch 1 is off and Switch 2 is on?

28. Why will chalk dust sprinkled on a plastic sheet placed over a bar magnet **NOT** show the shape of the magnetic field?

Process Skills Review

29. You **observe** that the north pole and south pole of two magnets attract each other when there is a piece of paper between them. What can you **infer** about magnetic fields and paper?

30. **Plan a simple investigation** to show the results of wrapping more coils of wire around a core. Be sure to include a description of the observations you would make and the conclusions you might draw. Use the following materials: a battery, a long piece of insulated copper wire with the ends stripped, an iron nail, a pile of paper clips.

31. Suppose you observe in the investigation you planned for Question 30 that the magnet picks up 5 paper clips with 10 coils of wire, 10 paper clips with 20 coils of wire, and 15 with 30 coils of wire. What would you **predict** will happen when you test the electromagnet with 40 coils of wire? How could you test your prediction?

Performance Assessment

Make a Circuit

Make a diagram of a parallel circuit with wires, three light bulbs, and two batteries. Show where to put a switch to turn all the lights off and on. Explain why you chose that switch location. Build and test the circuit.

Motion— Forces at Work

Vocabulary Preview

position
motion
frame of reference
relative motion
speed
force
newton
acceleration
gravity
weight
friction

There are forces acting all around you. When you write a letter, gravity holds the desk and you to the floor. Friction between your fingers and the pen keeps the pen upright. Gravity brings the ink to the pen's tip. The speed with which you move the pen determines how fast the letters are formed!

Fast Fact

You probably think that when you ice-skate, you are sliding on the ice. But ice without any water on top isn't very slippery. Warm air in the skating rink makes a thin layer of water. The water reduces friction between the ice and the skates, and you glide across the rink like a pro!

On the bottoms of their feet, geckos have hairs that increase friction. These tiny hairs let the lizards grip very smooth surfaces, even glass!

Friction slows a car when a driver brakes. It takes about 1.5 seconds for an alert driver to react to an emergency. It takes even longer to stop the car after the driver brakes. This table shows how far a car travels while a driver is reacting and braking and the total distance it takes to stop.

Car Braking

Speed (mi/hr)	A Reaction Distance (ft)	B Braking Distance (ft)	Total Stopping Distance [A+B]
20	44	25	69
30	66	57	123
40	88	101	189
50	110	158	268
60	132	227	359
70	154	310	464

LESSON 1

What Is Motion?

In this lesson, you can . . .

 INVESTIGATE giving directions.

 LEARN ABOUT motion and speed.

 LINK to math, writing, language arts, and technology.

Giving Directions

Activity Purpose When you give directions to get to a place, you tell someone when to turn and where to move. So, giving directions is a way to describe movement and position. For example, you might tell a new neighbor how to get to the grocery store, or you might tell a visiting family member how to find the school office. In this investigation you will write directions to get to a place you have chosen in your school.

Materials
- paper
- pencil

Activity Procedure

1 Choose a place in the school, such as a water fountain or an exit door. A person going there should have to make several turns. Tell your teacher the place you chose.

▲ Do you think the pitcher has thrown a fastball or a curveball? *Fast* and *curve* describe the movement of a ball. How else can you describe the motion of the ball?

2 After your teacher has approved your place, start walking to it. As you walk, **record** where and how you are moving. For example, you might include the distance you walk, about how long it takes for each part of the trip, where you turn, and any landmarks you use to tell where you are. (Picture A)

3 Go back to your classroom. On a separate sheet of paper, write directions to the place you chose. Use your notes to add details about time, distance, and position. Don't name the place on the directions page. Give the directions to a classmate and ask him or her to follow them. (Picture B)

4 When your partner comes back, talk about any problems he or she had with your directions. Underline the parts of the directions that caused the problems.

5 Walk with your partner as he or she follows the directions again. Decide together how to make the directions clearer. **Record** the reasons for any changes.

6 Switch roles with your partner and repeat Steps 1–5.

Picture A

Picture B

Draw Conclusions

1. How did your partner know where to start following the directions?

2. How did your partner know how far to walk, which direction to walk, and where to turn?

3. **Scientists at Work** Directions **communicate** the way to get from one place to another. **Compare** your directions to the procedure of an experiment.

Investigate Further Using your notes and directions, draw a map showing the way to the place you chose. Trade maps with a new partner. Is the map easier to use than written directions? Explain your answer.

Process Skill Tip

Often scientists repeat experiments that were done by others. So, it is important to **communicate** clearly all the parts of an experiment. These parts include how to do the experiment, the data collected, and the results and conclusions.

Motion

Changing Places

How do you tell someone where you are? Are you behind a desk? Under a light? Are you 2 meters (about 6 ft) to the left of the bookshelf? Each of these describes a certain place, or **position**. In the investigation, you chose a certain place. Then you wrote directions to tell someone how to move to get there, or how to change position. Good directions gave your partner a lot of ways to know his or her positions along the way and to find the next position.

As your partner followed your directions, he or she was in motion. **Motion** is any change of position. Your partner started in one position, moved to another, and kept changing position until he or she reached the final position—the place you chose. The photo below shows runners in motion around a track.

✔ **How do you know a runner is in motion?**

FIND OUT

- ways to describe motion
- what speed measures
- how to calculate speed

VOCABULARY

position
motion
frame of reference
relative motion
speed

In a race the position of the runner on the track changes from moment to moment. The race will be won by the person who moves, or changes position, fastest. ▼

Point of View

Look around you. Are you moving? You probably would say that you're not. You don't sense any change in your position. You answer questions about your motion by checking, or referring to, the things around you. Together, all the things around you that you can sense and use to describe motion make up your **frame of reference**.

You know that Earth is rotating on its axis and revolving around the sun. So, even when you sit at your desk, you actually *are* moving. But you can't sense that movement. You can't tell you are moving by using your frame of reference—the classroom and what you can sense from your seat.

Suppose an astronaut is watching your school from space far away from Earth. His or her answer about your movement on Earth will be different because the frame of reference is different. From space, the astronaut sees Earth rotate. Motion that is described based on a frame of reference

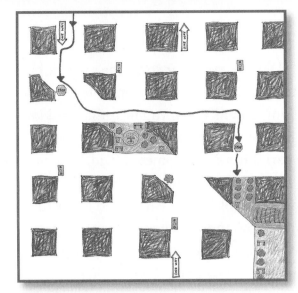

▲ To describe your position, you need a frame of reference. On a map you find your position by looking for landmarks or street names. How would you give directions to the park shown on the map? How would you check your position if you were following the directions?

is called **relative motion**. When you're sitting at your desk, your movement relative to the classroom is nothing. But your movement relative to the astronaut in space is very fast.

✔ **What is a frame of reference?**

▲ Jim watches Sarah and Rosa ride by on their bicycles. His frame of reference is what he sees by standing still on the sidewalk. Relative to him, the two girls are moving and the buildings and street are not moving.

Rosa's frame of reference is what she sees from her bike. Relative to Rosa, Sarah is not moving because the two girls are riding at the same speed. To Rosa, the buildings and street seem to be speeding by. Jim and Rosa describe Rosa's motion differently because they have different frames of reference.▼

Speed

Did you ever hear someone say that his or her house was only a five-minute bike ride from school? When you hear that, you know that the house and school are not too far apart. But what if someone said, "My house is only a five-minute spaceship ride away from school?" Then you would know that the house and school were very far apart. Why? You know that a spacecraft travels a lot faster than a bike. So it could go a lot farther in five minutes than a bike could.

Speed is one way to describe how fast something is moving. **Speed** is a measure of an object's change in position during a unit of time. For example, a racing swimmer has a speed of 1 meter (about 3 ft) per second. From this information, you know the swimmer is moving a distance of 1 meter (about 3 ft) during each second. So during 3 seconds, he or she will travel 3 meters (about 9 ft).

To find a swimmer's speed, you need two measurements. One measurement is change in position, or distance moved. Remember, you can't describe motion without a frame of reference. So you would measure how far the swimmer traveled from the end of the pool.

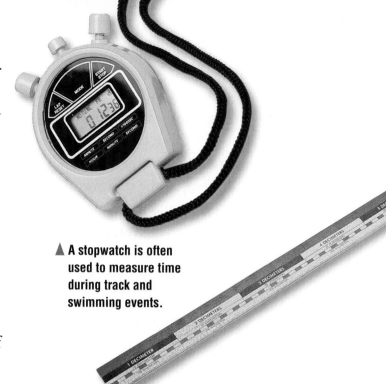

▲ A stopwatch is often used to measure time during track and swimming events.

How Fast Can You Go?

Activity	Distance (km)	Time (h)	Speed (km/h)
Flying in a jet plane	1000	1	1000
Riding in a car	240	3	80
Riding a bike	30	2	15
Walking	3	1	3

In a race each swimmer goes the same distance. The one who goes that distance in the least amount of time wins the race. That person has the greatest speed. ▼

◄ In some track and swimming events, distance is measured in meters.

The other measurement needed is time. You would start timing as the swimmer left the edge of the pool. The swimmer's speed is the distance moved divided by the time it took to move that distance. The table on page F42 shows how distance, time, and speed are related.

✓ **What is speed?**

Summary

Motion is any change from one position to another. A frame of reference is a point of view from which to describe motion. The same motion can look different from different frames of reference. Motion described from one frame of reference is called relative motion. Speed is a measure of motion. Speed describes the distance an object travels in a unit of time.

Review

1. What is position?
2. What is motion?
3. What is relative motion?
4. **Critical Thinking** Give two different frames of reference from which to describe a roller-coaster ride.
5. **Test Preparation** What is the speed of a cat that runs 6 meters in 3 seconds?

   A $\frac{1}{2}$ meter per second

   B 2 meters per second

   C 3 meters per second

   D 9 meters per second

LINKS

MATH LINK

Collect, Organize, and Display Data Use reference books to find the speeds of different land animals. Use a computer program such as *Graph Links* to make a bar graph of the speeds of some of the faster ones and some of the slower ones.

WRITING LINK

Expressive Writing—Poem Write a poem for your teacher. Describe the motion of running horses as you pass them while riding a passenger train.

LANGUAGE ARTS LINK

Moving Words Make a set of cards for matching. On one group of cards, write words describing motion, such as *fluttering*, *twirling*, and *dangling*. On another set of cards, write the names of different objects, such as *dog*, *leaf*, and *kite*. Turn the cards face down, and choose a card from each set. Turn the two cards face up. Write a sentence using the two words. Read your sentence to the class.

TECHNOLOGY LINK

Visit the Harcourt Learning Site for related links, activities, and resources.
www.harcourtschool.com

WELCOME TO THE LEARNING SITE

LESSON 2

What Effects Do Forces Have on Objects?

In this lesson, you can . . .

INVESTIGATE forces measured by spring scales.

LEARN ABOUT forces acting on objects.

LINK to math, writing, physical education, and technology.

Pairs of Forces Acting on Objects

Activity Purpose When you push a bicycle or a grocery cart, you expect it to move. But what happens if two people pull a grocery cart in opposite directions? What happens if they pull in the same direction? In this investigation you will **plan and conduct an investigation** to learn how pulling in two directions at the same time moves a toy car.

Materials

- safety goggles
- toy car
- 2 pieces of string, each 1 m long
- 2 spring scales
- ruler

Activity Procedure

CAUTION

1 **CAUTION** **Wear safety goggles to protect your eyes. The spring scale hooks or string may slip loose and fly up.** Work with a partner. Tie the ends of each string to the toy car. Pull on the string to make sure it won't come off easily. Attach a spring scale to each loop of string.

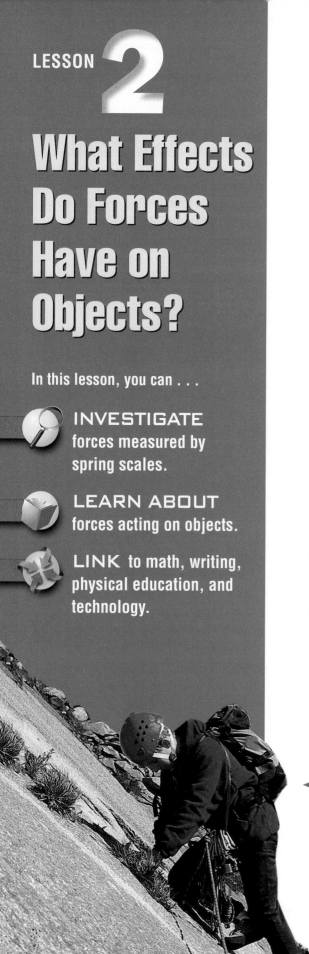

◀ This rock climber has strong arm and leg muscles that pull and push him up the rock face.

2 With a partner, try different ways and directions of pulling on the spring scales attached to the toy car. (Picture A)

3 **Plan a simple investigation.** Your goal is to **describe** how the toy car moves when two spring scales pull it at the same time. Plan to include a chart and a diagram to **record** your data and **observations.**

4 With your partner, carry out the investigation you planned.

Draw Conclusions

1. How did pulling in different directions affect the toy car?

2. How did pulling in the same direction affect the toy car?

3. **Scientists at Work** Scientists use what they know to help them **plan and conduct investigations**. What knowledge did you use to help you plan and conduct this investigation?

Investigate Further What will happen if you pull on the car with a third string and spring scale? **Form a hypothesis** that explains how the three forces interact. Then **plan and conduct an experiment** to test your hypothesis.

Process Skill Tip

To **plan and conduct an investigation**, scientists must first ask a good question. Then they must decide what they will observe or measure, what they will change, and what they will keep the same.

Forces

FIND OUT

- what a force is
- how an object moves when no force is acting on it
- how forces are added and subtracted

VOCABULARY

force
acceleration
newton

Pushes and Pulls

Think of all the times in a day you push or pull on something. You may push open doors, pull on a grocery cart, or push a pencil across paper. In the investigation you pulled a toy car. Every time you push or pull something, you use a force. A **force** is a push or a pull. Forces transfer energy. When you throw a ball, the force of your muscles moves your arm to push the ball into the air. When you pick up a book, the force of your muscles moves your arm to pull the book off the desk.

You're not the only source of forces. Other forces are pushing and pulling things all around you. The force put out by a car's engine turns the wheels to push the car down the road. The force of the wind pushes flags and tree branches, making them flap and rustle. The force of a magnet pulls it to a refrigerator door.

✔ **What is a force?**

◀ This archer pulls on the bowstring. When she lets go, the string will push the arrow away from the bow and toward the target.

F46

Starting Motion

Many of the things around you are probably motionless, or not moving. The books on your desk are motionless. So are the pictures on the wall. Objects stay in place unless a force starts them moving. If something is moving, you know that a force started it moving.

How a force affects an object depends on the object's mass. Suppose you push with equal force on a toy car and a wagon filled with books. When you stop pushing, the toy car will be moving much faster than the wagon. That is because the toy car has less mass than the wagon. A force affects an object with less mass more than it affects an object with more mass.

The force needed to start an object moving also depends on other forces that are acting on the object. Suppose your coat is fastened closed with Velcro. In that case the force needed to open your coat must be more than the force of the Velcro that's holding it closed.

▲ You have to pull to keep a sled moving uphill. If you stop pulling, the weight of the sled will pull it back down.

Once an object is moving, it moves until a force stops it. Sometimes it's easy to see where the stopping force comes from, such as when a soccer goalie stops a kicked ball. At other times, the stopping force is harder to name. You know that even if no other player stops a kicked soccer ball, the ball will stop rolling at some time. You can't see what stops the ball. It's a force called *friction* (FRIK•shuhn).

✔ **What do you have to do to start motion?**

◄ It's easy to start an empty grocery cart moving at a walking speed. After the cart is full, you must push it much harder to start it moving at a walking speed.

Changing direction is another kind of change in motion. It always takes a force to change the direction an object is moving. To turn, this in-line skater changes the angle of her skates. The skates push sideways to the left against the ground, and she skates around the curve. ▼

▲ When you stop, you change your motion. You slow down until you are not moving. It always takes a force to change motion. This in-line skater uses the force of the brake against the ground to make herself stop.

Changing Motion

It takes a force to start motion. Starting is a change from no motion to some motion. A force is needed to change motion in other ways, too. Speeding up, slowing down, turning, and stopping all are motion changes that need a force.

If you've ridden a bicycle on a smooth, level surface, you know that you can coast. Once you start moving, you can keep going for a while without pedaling. But to speed up, you have to pedal. The force of your feet pushing on the pedals speeds up the bicycle. To slow down or stop, you squeeze, or put force on, the brake handles.

Suppose you are riding a bicycle and want to turn left. You turn the handlebars to the left. The front wheel pushes sideways against the pavement and the bicycle moves left. If you were riding on icy pavement, turning would be harder. The front wheel couldn't push sideways against the pavement without slipping.

Starting and slowing to a stop are examples of changing speed. Turning is an example of changing direction. Starting, slowing, and turning are all accelerations. An **acceleration** (ak•sel•er•AY•shuhn) is any change in the speed or the direction of an object's motion. It always takes a force to cause an acceleration.

✔ **What is needed to make an object change its motion?**

Changing Speed

A larger force causes a larger acceleration. This means that the harder you push something, the more quickly it speeds up. When you pedal your bicycle harder, it goes faster. If you squeeze harder on the brake handles, you will stop faster.

Pushing for a longer time also causes a larger acceleration. If you get on a bicycle and pedal hard for 2 seconds, you will be moving slowly. If you pedal just as hard for 20 seconds, you will be moving much faster.

✔ **What is needed to give an object a greater acceleration?**

At the start of a race, the push of the bobsled team starts the bobsled moving. The push of the team increases the speed of the sled from 0 to 15 kilometers (about 10 mi) per hour.

Force accelerating bobsled

◄ As the bobsled slides down the curving course, its weight accelerates it bit by bit. The longer the bobsled moves down the hill, the faster it goes. The sled's final speed may be 145 kilometers (about 90 mi) per hour or more.

▲ Both dogs are pulling with the same force. The forces on the rope are balanced. There is no acceleration, and the rope doesn't move. The arrows stand for the forces. When you put them side by side, you can see they are balanced.

Adding Forces

Suppose you push on a box from one side and your friend pushes on it from the opposite side. What happens? If your friend pushes just as hard as you do, the box won't move. The forces are balanced. When all forces acting on an object are balanced, the motion of an object does not change. It does not accelerate.

If you push harder than your friend pushes, the box will move toward your friend. But if your friend pushes harder than you do, the box will move toward you.

When forces on an object are in opposite directions, you subtract the smaller force from the larger force. The force that remains will accelerate the object.

When two forces on an object are in the same direction, they add together. The force that results is in the same direction as the two forces and is larger than either of them. The photo below shows how forces can add together to move a piano easily.

✔ **What happens to an object when the forces acting on it are balanced?**

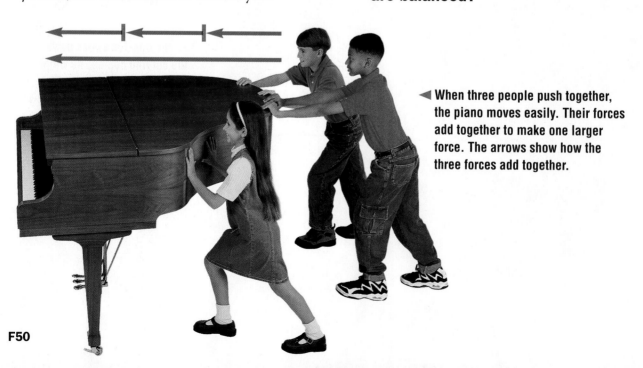

◄ When three people push together, the piano moves easily. Their forces add together to make one larger force. The arrows show how the three forces add together.

F50

Measuring Forces

You used spring scales in the investigation to help you observe the effects of two forces on a toy car. The numbers on the spring scale showed you the size of the force in units called newtons. The **newton** is the metric, or Système International (SI), unit of force. It's abbreviated as *N*. A newton is a small amount of force. It's about as much force as you need to lift a medium-sized apple.

A spring scale can show how accelerating an object depends on the object's mass. Suppose you hook a spring scale to an empty wagon. Then you take two steps to pull the wagon up to your walking speed. As you pull, the scale reads 10 N. Next, you put your dog in the wagon. Again, you take two steps to pull the wagon up to walking speed. This time the scale reads 20 N. Putting the dog in the wagon added mass. Because of the added mass, it took a larger force to accelerate the wagon to the same speed in the same amount of time.

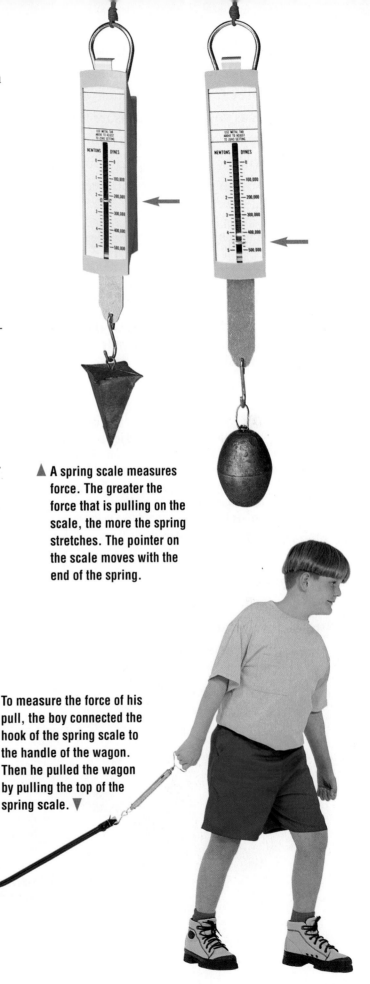

▲ A spring scale measures force. The greater the force that is pulling on the scale, the more the spring stretches. The pointer on the scale moves with the end of the spring.

To measure the force of his pull, the boy connected the hook of the spring scale to the handle of the wagon. Then he pulled the wagon by pulling the top of the spring scale. ▼

As its name suggests, a spring scale has a spring in it. When you pull on the scale, you stretch the spring. The pointer on the scale moves as you pull. To measure the force you are using, you have to be able to lift or pull on the spring scale. Holding the scale and pushing won't give you a reading on the scale.

Other kinds of scales also measure forces. You've probably seen a bathroom scale or the scale at a grocery store checkout lane.

✓ **What does the stretch of a spring scale measure?**

Two Scales

These are two other kinds of scales. They also measure force, but they work differently from a simple spring scale.

This is a dial spring scale. Dial spring scales are often found in the produce sections of grocery stores. The push of an object placed in the pan stretches a spring that has a gear attached to it. As the gear moves down, it causes a needle to turn. The tip of the needle points to the amount of force with which the object pushes on the pan. ▶

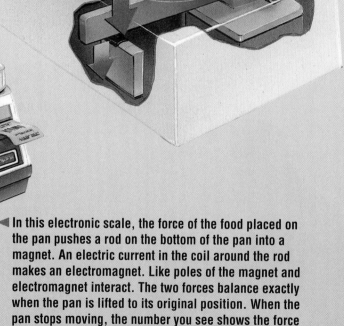

◀ In this electronic scale, the force of the food placed on the pan pushes a rod on the bottom of the pan into a magnet. An electric current in the coil around the rod makes an electromagnet. Like poles of the magnet and electromagnet interact. The two forces balance exactly when the pan is lifted to its original position. When the pan stops moving, the number you see shows the force of the food on the pan.

▲ Scales can also be very large. This scale measures the weight of trucks full of gravel and asphalt.

Summary

A force is a push or a pull. Starting, stopping, slowing down, and turning are all changes in motion, or kinds of acceleration. An object does not accelerate unless a force acts on it. Forces can add together, subtract, or balance each other. When all the forces on an object are balanced, it does not accelerate. Forces are measured in newtons (N).

Review

1. What is a force?
2. What is the name of the SI unit of force?
3. What is acceleration?
4. **Critical Thinking** What happens to a door if you push on one side and someone else pushes with the same amount of force on the other side?
5. **Test Preparation** What happens when you are riding your bicycle on a smooth, level surface and you stop pedaling?
   A You stop right away.
   B You go faster.
   C You slowly slow down.
   D You turn to the right.

LINKS

MATH LINK

Draw a Picture to Solve a Problem
Two students are pushing on a piano. One student can push with a force of 30 newtons. The other can push with a force of 50 newtons. What is the greatest force they can use to push on the piano? What is the smallest force that they can put on the piano if they both push hard?

WRITING LINK

Expressive Writing—Song Lyrics
Choose a tune you know. Then write words to go with that tune. The words should describe for a younger child ways to use forces to move an elephant from the zoo to your house. You might want to include a verse about what you will do with the elephant once you get it home.

PHYSICAL EDUCATION LINK

Sports and Motion Make a list of at least five different sports. Then make a chart to identify objects that change motion while each sport is being played.

TECHNOLOGY LINK

Learn more about forces and accelerations by viewing *Coaster Physics* on the **Harcourt Science Newsroom Video.**

What Are Some Forces in Nature?

In this lesson, you can . . .

 INVESTIGATE forces on a sliding box.

 LEARN ABOUT four different types of forces.

 LINK to math, writing, art, and technology.

INVESTIGATE

Forces on a Sliding Box

Activity Purpose
Have you ever slipped on a patch of ice? To make ice on a sidewalk less slippery, you can put sand on it. In this investigation you will **measure** the force that you need to slide a box across several different materials. You will **order** the measurements and use them to **compare** the materials.

Materials
- shoe box
- spring scale
- books

Activity Procedure

1 Make a table to **record** your **observations.**

2 Put the hook of the spring scale through the two openings on the end of the box. Place several books in the box. (Picture A)

3 Use the spring scale to slowly drag the box across the top of a desk or table. Be sure to pull with the spring scale straight out from the side of the box. Practice this step several times until you can pull the box at a steady, slow speed. (Picture B)

◀ The force of gravity is pulling this snowboarder down the hill. The force of friction is holding him back. But the snowboard is made to slide on the snow with as little friction as possible. So its speed is quite fast.

Picture A

Picture B

4 When you are ready, **measure** the force of your pull as you drag the box. **Record** the force measurement and the surface on which you dragged the box. **Observe** the texture of the surface.

5 Repeat Steps 3 and 4, dragging the box across other surfaces, such as the classroom floor, carpet, tile, and cement. **Predict** the force needed to drag the box on each surface.

Draw Conclusions

1. Make a new table. In this table, list the forces you used in order from the smallest to the largest. What was the least amount of force you used?

2. In your new table, write the name of each surface next to the force you used on it. On which surface did you use the greatest amount of force?

3. How did a surface affect the force needed to drag the shoe box across it?

4. **Scientists at Work** After scientists gather data, they often put it in some kind of **order** to help them understand their results. How did putting your data in order help you in this investigation?

Investigate Further **Predict** how much force it would take to pull the shoe box across a patch of ice. If possible, find a place, and test your prediction.

> ### Process Skill Tip
>
> When scientists measure many things in the same way, they usually put the data in **order.** Often they start with the smallest measurement and end with the largest. This helps them compare data and makes any patterns easier to see.

Kinds of Force

Gravity

FIND OUT

- what gravity is
- what holds atoms together
- how friction slows down motion

VOCABULARY

gravity
weight
friction

If you pick up a rock and then drop it, it will fall to the ground. The rock can't move by itself. A force is needed to move it. The force that pulls things toward Earth is called gravity. **Gravity** (GRAV•ih•tee) is a force that pulls all objects toward each other. The size of the force depends on the mass of the objects and how far apart they are. The pull between objects that have a large mass is stronger than the pull between objects that have a small mass. For example, the mass of Earth is large, so its pull on you is strong. But you have much less mass than Earth has, so the pull of your gravity on other objects is much too small to notice.

The greater the distance between objects, the weaker the pull of gravity is. The pull of gravity is strong between Earth and everything near its surface, including you. Space satellites orbit far from Earth. The pull between Earth and a satellite orbiting over one place on Earth's equator is small. It is only about $\frac{2}{100}$ of what the pull would be at Earth's surface.

✔ **What is gravity?**

The force of gravity between the sun and Earth pulls them toward each other. The pull between Earth and the sun holds Earth in its orbit around the sun. ▼

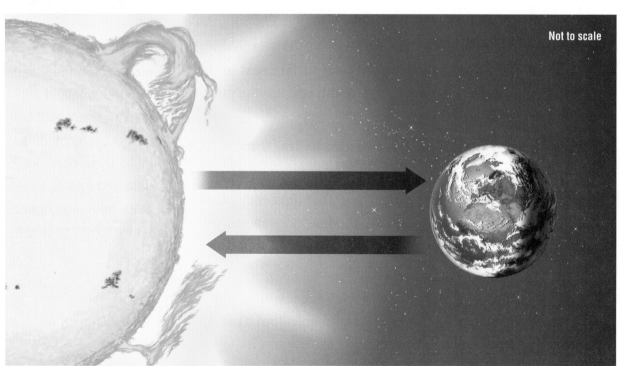

Not to scale

The girl's weight is a measure of the force of gravity between Earth and the girl. ▼

Weight on Planets in Our Solar System	
Planet	**Weight**
Mercury	102 N (23 lb)
Venus	245 N (54 lb)
Earth	270 N (60 lb)
Mars	102 N (23 lb)
Jupiter	638 N (142 lb)
Saturn	247 N (55 lb)
Uranus	240 N (53 lb)
Neptune	304 N (68 lb)
Pluto	18 N (4 lb)

◄ This arrow stands for the girl's weight on Earth.

The force of gravity between Mars and the girl is about one-third the force of gravity between Earth and the girl. On Mars her weight would be about one-third her weight on Earth. ►

Weight

How many times have you had your weight measured? You probably know what your weight is now. **Weight** is a measure of the force of gravity on an object. Your weight is a measure of the force of gravity between you and Earth.

If you go to a place where the force of gravity is different, your weight will be different, too. The force of gravity on the moon is less than on Earth. That's mostly because the moon has less mass than Earth. The moon's gravity is about one-sixth of Earth's gravity. So on the moon your weight would be one-sixth of your weight on Earth. The force of gravity near Jupiter is much larger than it is near Earth. On Jupiter your weight would be more than twice what it is on Earth.

✔ **Why would you weigh less on the moon than you do on Earth?**

F57

Friction

In the investigation you pulled a shoe box filled with books across a desktop. As you were pulling the shoe box forward, another force was pulling it back. That force was friction. **Friction** (FRIK•shuhn) is a force that keeps objects that are touching each other from sliding past each other easily. As you observed in the investigation, the rougher a surface is, the more friction it has.

Sometimes friction is useful. Without friction, walking on a sidewalk would be like slipping on perfectly smooth ice. Friction also can stop motion. When you use a bicycle brake, pieces of rubber rub against the wheel rims. The friction between the rubber and the rims slows and stops the wheels. The harder you squeeze, the faster the bicycle stops.

Often people want to make the force of friction smaller. Friction can wear away machine parts that rub against each other. To reduce friction, people put oil on the machine parts to make them more slippery. This is why car engines need oil.

✔ **What is friction?**

When the wheel of this grinder touches the sculpture, it drags away little pieces of metal. Some of the energy from the grinder makes the metal red-hot. ▼

▲ An in-line skater pushes the heel stop of the skate against the ground to slow down or stop. Friction reduces the skater's speed.

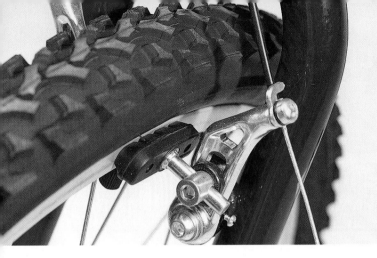

LINKS

MATH LINK

Solve a Two-Step Problem A rock that weighs 18 newtons on Earth weighs 3 newtons on the moon. What would a rock that weighs 12 newtons on Earth weigh on the moon?

WRITING LINK

Expressive Writing—Friendly Letter Suppose you are an astronaut who has landed on a planet that has a force of gravity two times as strong as Earth has. Write a letter to a friend on Earth, describing how it feels to walk and to lift tools.

ART LINK

See the Force Look at the things around you. Choose one object and then think of the different forces that are acting on it. Make a drawing, painting, or sculpture that shows the object and the forces acting on it.

TECHNOLOGY LINK

Learn about friction, gravity, and motion by investigating *Build a Model Race Car* on **Harcourt Science Explorations CD-ROM.**

▲ The friction caused by the brake rubbing against the bicycle wheel stops the wheel.

Summary

Forces in nature include gravity and friction. Gravity keeps you on Earth. Friction is a force that keeps things from sliding past each other easily.

Review

1. Would you expect the force of gravity one kilometer above the moon to be stronger or weaker than the force of gravity at its surface?

2. If the mass of Earth doubled, how would your weight change?

3. What is the force between two objects that keeps one object from sliding past the other easily?

4. **Critical Thinking** Where do you think the pull of gravity is stronger—at the surface of Earth or at the surface of the sun? Explain.

5. **Test Preparation** The direction of the force of friction on a book sliding to the right on a table is —

   A down
   B to the left
   C to the right
   D up

High-Speed HUMAN-POWERED VEHICLES

Engineers who develop high-tech bicycles work with forces, accelerations, and friction every day. Their job is to build Human Powered Vehicles (HPVs) that are as fast and as easy to ride as possible.

Cheetah

HUMAN POWERED VEHICLE

What's the big idea?

Most people in the United States who ride bikes do it for fun, not because they need them for transportation. When you want to travel long distances quickly, you often go in a car. But teams of scientists and engineers who work on HPVs have developed bikes that can go even faster than some cars.

How fast are they?

One of the best-known HPVs is called the Cheetah. It was built by a team of college students at the University of California. In 1992, scientists recorded the Cheetah traveling as fast as 112 kilometers (70 mi) per hour. The fastest that most regular bikes can go is 40–48 kilometers (25–30 mi) per hour.

The fastest HPV that has been built so far is the Ultimate Bike. Because its engineers understood ideas such as friction, force, and weight, they were able to design a bike that can reach speeds as fast as 332.64 kilometers (206.7 mi) per hour. The Ultimate Bike is made from the same super-lightweight material used in jet planes. But even though it weighs only about $4\frac{1}{2}$ kilograms (about 10 pounds), the Ultimate Bike is stronger than any bike made from metal.

How do they work?

You've probably noticed from the photos that these bikes don't look like the bikes you see in your neighborhood. That's because they need to be built differently to reach such high speeds. For example, most HPVs have a gear system that's different from the one on regular bikes. The front crank that is turned by the pedals is much bigger than the crank on most bikes. This allows small movements of the pedals to make the wheels turn a large distance quickly.

Wind resistance can greatly reduce bicycle speed. That's why these HPVs have the pedals in front of the rider. The rider sits close to the ground, so less of his or her body is hit by the wind. See if you can feel the wind resistance the next time you ride a bicycle. What can you do safely to reduce this resistance?

You probably won't see HPVs like these in a bike store soon. But the problems HPV scientists and engineers are solving may make ordinary bicycles faster and easier to ride.

THINK ABOUT IT

1. How could an HPV be useful to the average person?
2. In addition to that of an engineer, what are some jobs where ideas like acceleration, force, and friction are important?

CAREERS
BICYCLE MECHANIC

What They Do Bicycle mechanics usually work for bike shops or sporting goods stores. They repair broken bikes and build new ones. HPVs like the Cheetah and the Ultimate Bike need mechanics to keep them running.

Education and Training Most bike shops will train their workers to be mechanics. Some high schools offer bike repair classes.

WEB LINK
For Science and Technology updates, visit the Harcourt Internet site.
www.harcourtschool.com

Ellen Ochoa

ASTRONAUT

"Only you put limitations on yourself about what you can achieve, so don't be afraid to reach for the stars."

Ellen Ochoa puts no limitations on herself. She became the first Hispanic woman in space. Chosen in 1990 by the National Aeronautics and Space Administration, Ochoa was a mission specialist on the 9-day-long *Discovery* mission in April 1993. On this mission she studied the sun and Earth's atmosphere to find out how the sun affects Earth's climate. She also flew on an 11-day mission in November 1994. She has spent almost 500 hours in space.

The most challenging part of space travel is remembering details. Every astronaut is trained to run all shuttle systems, such as computer, communication, air and water, and other equipment. All astronauts learn about the experiments and other jobs that are part of a shuttle mission. Ochoa says that astronauts must work very hard in space, because they have little time.

Ochoa dreams of helping to build a space station. She thinks it is needed for human exploration in space to advance. For two years, she directed all Astronaut Office support for the International Space Station program.

Ochoa believes that education is key to success in life. She learned this from her mother. Ochoa believes students, especially girls, should study math and science. Another role model for Ochoa was Sally Ride, the first American woman in space. "Sally made it possible for anyone to become an astronaut," Ochoa has said. Ride was in space when Ochoa was in college and first thinking of becoming an astronaut.

THINK ABOUT IT

1. How could studying math and science be helpful to you?
2. Who in your life has taught you that education is important?

Model of completed International Space Station

OBSERVING MOTION

How does motion result from changing position?

Materials

- pad of small self-stick notes
- ruler
- pencil

Procedure

1 Hold the pad so that the sticky band is across the top. On the first note, draw a dot 1 cm from the bottom of the pad and 1 mm from the left side. Lift the note, but do not remove it from the pad.

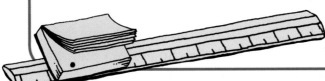

2 On the second note, draw a dot 1 cm from the bottom and 2 mm from the left side.

3 On separate notes, continue drawing dots, each one 1 mm to the right of the previous one until the last dot is at the right side. Remove any notes that were not used.

4 Hold the note pad by the top, and flip the pages with your thumb. Observe the dots.

Draw Conclusions

How do the dots show a change in position over time? What happens if you flip the pages faster?

MARBLES ON A RAMP

Which marbles go faster?

Materials

- masking tape
- 2 metersticks
- books
- meter tape or ruler
- 10 marbles
- stopwatch

Procedure

1 Tape the two metersticks together at a right-angle as shown. Prop up one end of the meter-sticks with books to make a ramp.

2 Put the meter tape on the floor, with the zero mark at the low end

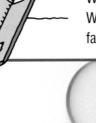

of the ramp. Make a table for your data, with columns labeled *Starting Position* and *Time*.

3 Roll the marbles down the ramp one at a time. Start the marbles from different positions on the ramp. In your table, record the starting position for each marble.

4 Use the stopwatch to measure the time it takes the marble to travel the length of the meter tape. Record the time in your table. Graph your results.

Draw Conclusions

What force pulled the marbles down the ramp? Which height made the speed of the marbles the fastest as they left the ramp? The slowest?

Vocabulary Review

Use the terms below to complete the sentences. The page numbers in ( ) tell you where to look in the chapter if you need help.

position (F40)   **acceleration** (F48)

motion (F40)   **newton** (F51)

frame of reference (F41) **gravity** (F56)

relative motion (F41)   **weight** (F57)

speed (F42)   **friction** (F58)

force (F46)

1. The force that pulls all objects together is called ____.

2. Meters per second is a unit of ____, or the distance an object travels in a unit of time.

3. A certain place is called ____.

4. A ____ is a push or a pull.

5. A unit called a ____ is used to measure pulls and pushes.

6. ____ is a change in position.

7. Your ____ is the measure of the force of gravity on you.

8. A ____ is a point of view from which to describe motion.

9. Stopping your bike is an example of an ____.

10. Motion described from a frame of reference is called ____.

11. ____ is a force that keeps objects that are touching each other from sliding past each other easily.

Connect Concepts

Match the following effects with their causes.

Cause	Effect
12. gravity	a. acceleration
13. objects sliding past each other	b. a spring scale moves
14. unbalanced force on object	c. friction
15. no force on moving object	d. pulls any two objects toward each other
16. balanced forces on object at rest	e. change in object's position
17. weight	f. no change in object's speed
18. motion	g. no movement of object

Check Understanding

Write the letter of the best choice.

19. If you are standing in an elevator that is moving up at a steady speed of 1 meter per second, your motion relative to the elevator is at a speed of —

   A 0 meters per second

   B 1 meter per second down

   C 1 meter per second up

   D 2 meters per second up

20. Each of the following is an example of acceleration **EXCEPT** —

   F resting

   G starting

   H stopping

   J turning

21. The _____ pulls the moon toward Earth.

   A electric force

   B friction

   C force of gravity

   D magnetic force

Critical Thinking

22. Suppose you are riding in a car and you pass a truck going in the same direction you are. You can easily read the words printed on the side of the truck. But then the same truck passes you going the same speed in the opposite direction. This time the words are hard to read. Why?

23. Your push on a hockey puck moving toward you stops it. What will the same push do to a hockey puck moving away from you?

24. A monkey that weighs 270 newtons is hanging from the branch of a tree. What is the size and direction of the monkey's force on the tree branch?

Process Skills Review

25. A student measured the force needed to pull a wagon across a wood floor, a heavy rug, and grass. He decided to **communicate** the results with a bar graph. The three bars on the graph each had the same width but different heights. What did the height of a bar show?

26. Look at the data in the table on page F57. How is the data **ordered**? Think of another possible order, and put the data in that order. Explain the new order.

27. A student decided to find out if a change in speed changes the force of friction. Help her **plan an investigation** to find this out. Include tips she could use as she **conducts** the **investigation**.

Performance Assessment

Force Drawing

Use a spring scale to measure the force needed to pull a book across a desktop at a steady speed. Identify and give the direction of three forces on the book as it slides. Make and label a drawing to show the forces.

F65

Simple Machines

In an old comedy movie, movers try to get a piano into a fifth-floor apartment. First the piano rolls down a truck ramp and on down a hill. Then they use pulleys to lift the piano into the apartment through a window, and the piano crashes back to the ground. What makes all this comedy possible? Acting talent and simple machines!

Fast Fact

With a long enough lever your weight could lift almost any object! In fact, with a lever 4800 meters long you could lift a whale!

Lever Lengths

Object One Meter from Fulcrum	Mass of Object (kg)	Your Distance from Fulcrum (m)
Student	27	1
Adult	68	2.5
30 Friends	810	30
Elephant	4995	185
Whale	129,600	4800

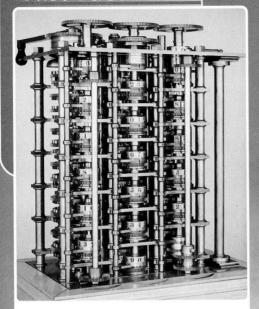

The first computer was designed by Charles Babbage in 1832. It was to be entirely mechanical and would use more than a thousand levers!

Can you guess what kind of machine was first called a wooden ox or a gliding horse? This useful machine, made up of two levers connected by a wheel, lets one person carry a load that would normally require two. The machine was invented around A.D. 200 by the Chinese. It's a wheelbarrow!

This drawbridge in Mystic, Connecticut, is a large lever. The weight of the bridge is balanced by the large concrete blocks at the top on the right.

How Does a Lever Help Us Do Work?

In this lesson, you can . . .

INVESTIGATE how one kind of lever works.

LEARN ABOUT how levers help us do work.

LINK to math, writing, music, and technology.

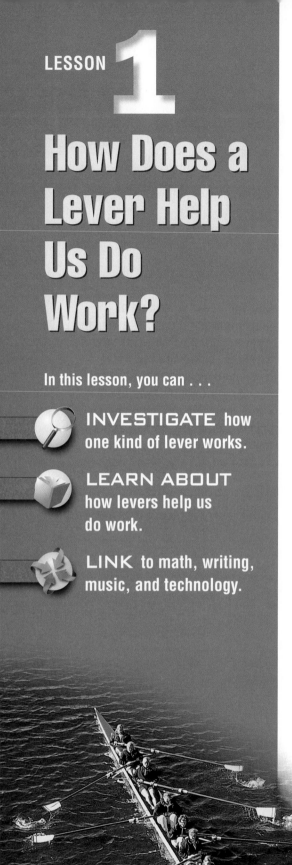

Experimenting with a Lever

Activity Purpose You may have played on a seesaw, or teeter-totter. A seesaw is a type of lever. A *lever* is a bar that turns on a point that doesn't move. In a seesaw the board is the bar and the center pipe is the point that doesn't move. A person sits near each end of the board. Each person takes a turn lifting a weight (the other person) at the other end of the board. As the people take turns using their legs and weight to lift each other, the board goes up and down. But what if the weight you were trying to lift were in the middle of the lever instead of at the end? In this investigation you will **observe** and **measure** to find out what happens.

Materials
- 2 wooden rulers
- 2 identical rubber bands, long
- safety goggles

Activity Procedure

1 **CAUTION** **Put on your safety goggles.** Put a rubber band 2 cm from each end of the ruler. One band should be at the 2-cm mark, and the other should be at the 28-cm mark.

◀ A boat oar is a lever—a type of simple machine made up of a bar and a point on which the bar moves. The wood oar is the bar. It moves around a point, called an oarlock, on the side of the boat.

Positions and Rubber Band Lengths

Finger Position	Observations	Length of Rubber Band on 2-cm Mark	Length of Rubber Band on 28-cm Mark
15-cm mark			
17-cm mark			
19-cm mark			
21-cm mark			

2 Have a partner lift the ruler by holding the rubber bands. Place your index finger at the 15-cm mark, and press down just enough to stretch the rubber bands. Your partner should lift hard enough on both rubber bands to keep the ruler level. (Picture A)

3 Have a third person **measure** the lengths of the two bands. **Record** your **observations** and measurements in a chart like the one above.

Picture A

4 Move your finger to the 17-cm mark. Your partner should keep the ruler level. Again **measure** the length of the rubber bands, and **record** your **observations** and measurements.

5 Repeat Step 4, this time with your finger at the 19-cm mark and then the 21-cm mark.

Draw Conclusions

1. Describe what happened to the ruler each time you moved your finger away from the center of it.

2. **Compare** the ruler and rubber bands to a seesaw. What was the ruler? What were the forces of the rubber bands?

3. **Scientists at Work** Look at the **measurements** you recorded. How do they support your other observations? Is there a pattern?

Investigate Further For the same ruler setup, **predict** what will happen if you put your finger on the 9-cm mark. Try it and see if your prediction is correct.

Process Skill Tip

Measuring is one type of observation. Measurements can sometimes more clearly show a pattern. They also are a good way to communicate to other people what you observed.

F69

Levers

FIND OUT

- what a simple machine is
- how a lever works
- what *work* means in science

VOCABULARY

simple machine
lever
fulcrum
effort force
work

Parts of a Lever

You may picture a machine, such as a washing machine or a sewing machine, as a device that has many parts. But these machines are built from smaller parts that are also machines. The basic machines that make up other machines are called **simple machines**. There are six simple machines. They are the lever, pulley, wheel and axle, inclined plane, screw, and wedge. All these machines help us move things by changing the size of the force applied, the direction of the force, or both at once.

One simple machine is the lever. As you saw in the investigation, a **lever** is made up of a bar that turns on a fixed point. The fixed point, or one that doesn't move, is called the **fulcrum** (FUHL•krem).

When you push or pull a lever, you put a force, called the **effort force**, on one side of the bar. This force causes the bar to turn on the fulcrum. The other end of the bar moves. The resulting force on that end is what you use to move a load, or do work. In the investigation, the length of each stretched rubber band showed the force on each end of the lever.

✔ **What are the parts of a lever?**

If both the performer's feet are the same distance away from the fulcrum, it's easy for him to stay balanced. ▶

This diagram shows how the performer is balancing on the lever. The blue arrow stands for the effort force, the red arrow is the resulting force, and the small dot is the fulcrum. The effort and resulting forces are balanced, so the lever doesn't move. ▼

Effort force

Resulting force

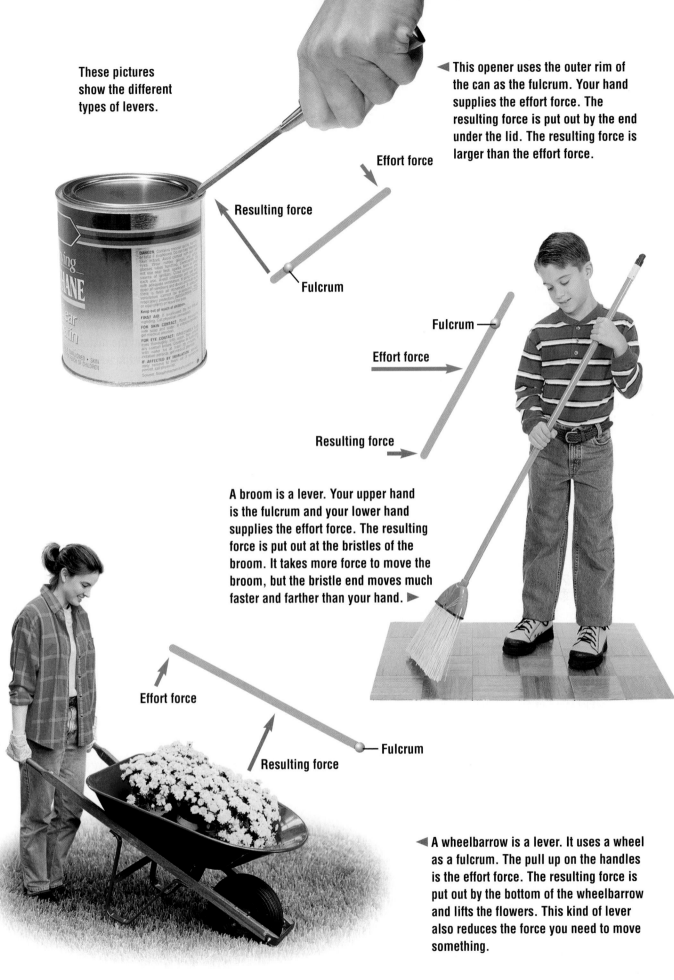

These pictures show the different types of levers.

◄ This opener uses the outer rim of the can as the fulcrum. Your hand supplies the effort force. The resulting force is put out by the end under the lid. The resulting force is larger than the effort force.

Effort force

Resulting force

Fulcrum

Fulcrum

Effort force

Resulting force

A broom is a lever. Your upper hand is the fulcrum and your lower hand supplies the effort force. The resulting force is put out at the bristles of the broom. It takes more force to move the broom, but the bristle end moves much faster and farther than your hand. ►

Effort force

Resulting force

Fulcrum

◄ A wheelbarrow is a lever. It uses a wheel as a fulcrum. The pull up on the handles is the effort force. The resulting force is put out by the bottom of the wheelbarrow and lifts the flowers. This kind of lever also reduces the force you need to move something.

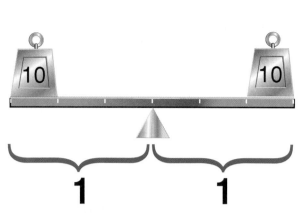

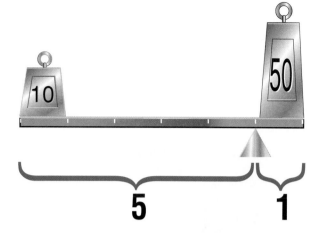

▲ A lever is often compared to a seesaw. If the weights are the same and the distances from the fulcrum are the same, the seesaw balances.

▲ Changing the position of the fulcrum changes the balance of the lever. Now a small effort force makes a larger resulting force. The distance from the fulcrum to the 10-newton weight is five times larger than the distance from the fulcrum to the 50-newton weight.

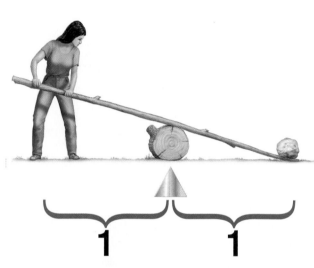

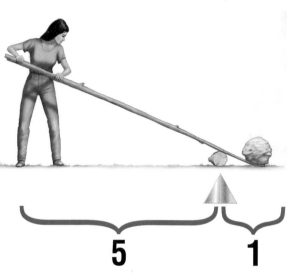

▲ The balanced lever above has the fulcrum in the center. If you move one end of the branch down, the other end moves up the same distance. An effort force of 10 newtons lifts a rock weighing 10 newtons.

▲ When this lever moves, the long end travels five times farther down than the short end travels up. To lift a 50-newton rock would take an effort force of only 10 newtons. But you have to push five times farther down than the rock is lifted up.

Levers and Forces

The kind of lever shown above changes the direction of the force applied to it. A force down on one side pushes the other side up. On a seesaw the weight of a person on the high end pushes that end down. This lifts the person sitting on the other end.

When the fulcrum of this kind of lever is not in the middle of the bar, a light weight on the long side can balance a heavy weight on the short side.

On a seesaw you can balance a heavier person if the fulcrum is closer to him or her. Your smaller weight is on the long side of the lever. It balances the larger weight on the other end.

✔ **How does a lever change the force applied to it?**

Levers in Tools

Many hand tools are levers. A pry bar is a lever that has a long handle and a short end for prying. A small force on the handle becomes a much greater force on the prying end. Sewing scissors have long, wedge-shaped blades and short handles. The fulcrum is the bolt in the middle. A large movement of the handles causes a small movement of the blades close to the bolt. Fingernail scissors have long handles and short blades. They make it easier to cut hard fingernails.

✔ **Name three tools that include levers.**

Pliers (PLY•erz) are formed by two levers that are connected at a fulcrum. A small squeeze on the long handles makes a much greater force at the tips. ▼

Fulcrum

Resulting force

Effort force

THE INSIDE STORY

Piano Keys

A piano makes a sound when the part called a hammer hits a string that then vibrates. The force on a piano key moves through a series of levers to cause the string to be hit. The levers form a compound machine, a machine made up of two or more simple machines.

Here's how it works.

❶ Pushing a piano key down lifts up the other end of a long lever (Lever 1). The direction of the effort force on the key is changed.

❷ Lever 1 pushes up on Lever 2. The direction of the force stays the same, but Lever 2 moves farther than Lever 1. This is because of the location of the fulcrum of Lever 2.

❸ Lever 2 pushes up on Lever 3. A padded hammer is on the end of Lever 3. Again, because of the position of its fulcrum, Lever 3 increases the distance the hammer moves. The hammer moves up fast and strikes the string. Then the hammer is caught as it bounces off the string, before it hits the string again.

❹ A pianist moves each finger only a small distance—about 1 centimeter (less than $\frac{1}{2}$ in.)—to produce a strong hit on a piano string.

F73

Work

Machines are used to do work. You may think that as you read this sentence, you are doing work, but a scientist would say you're not. In science, the word *work* has a special meaning. **Work** is done on an object when a force moves the object through a distance. The force and motion *must* be in the same direction. By this definition, thinking isn't work. Just holding a book isn't doing work on the book. But lifting a book is doing work on the book. Carrying a basketball isn't doing work on the basketball. This is because the force holding the ball up and its motion aren't in the same direction. Shooting the basketball, however, is doing work on the ball.

Levers help you do work. You could pick up a heavy rock using just your arms, or you could use a lever to help you. Either way the same amount of work gets done. The rock is lifted the same distance.

Work can be measured and described mathematically. To find the work done on an object, multiply the force used to move the object by the distance the object moves.

$$Work = Force \times distance$$

Here's the work done to lift a 10-newton rock 2 meters.

$Work = 10 \text{ N} \times 2 \text{ m}$

$Work = 20 \text{ N-m (newton-meters)}$

✔ **In science, when is work done?**

In this type of lever, the amount of work done is about the same on either side of the fulcrum. It takes only a small force to push down the long end, but that end moves through a large distance. On the short end, a large force pushes up, but that end moves only a small distance. ▼

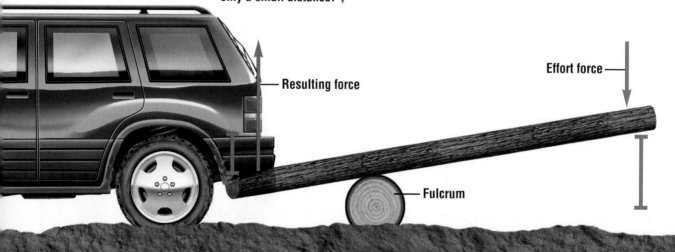

Resulting force

Effort force

Fulcrum

◀ At work or at play? You may think that the adult dressed in black is working and the students are playing. Look again, but this time use a scientist's definition of *work*. The supervisor isn't moving any objects. So she isn't doing any work on anything. The students to the right, on the other hand, are applying forces to lift a ball. So they are actually doing work on the ball.

Summary

The basic machines that make up all other machines are simple machines. A lever is a simple machine that changes the direction or size of a force. Work is done on an object when a force moves an object through a distance.

Review

1. What are the parts of a lever?
2. How does a pry bar help you do work?
3. What is work?
4. **Critical Thinking** Why do you think it is important that the bar of a lever not bend?
5. **Test Prep** An example of a lever is a —
   A wheelbarrow
   B wheel
   C screw
   D wrench

LINKS

MATH LINK

Measure Length Measure and compare the lengths of the effort force and resulting force arrows shown with the wheelbarrow on page F71. Which arrow is longer? About how many times as long is it? Which force is greater—the effort force or resulting force? How many times as great?

WRITING LINK

Informative Writing—Description
Some apes, including chimpanzees and orangutans, use levers. Other animals, including crows and sea otters, also use very simple tools. Find an example of how an animal uses a tool. Write an article describing how the animal uses the tool to help meet its needs.

MUSIC LINK

Instrument Keys Many musical instruments use keys, including almost all the woodwinds and many of the brasses. As with piano keys, the keys on these instruments are levers. Choose an instrument and find out how the keys work the levers. What do the levers do?

GO ONLINE TECHNOLOGY LINK

Learn more about levers and other simple machines by visiting this Internet site.
www.scilinks.org/harcourt

SCi LINKS
THE WORLD'S A CLICK AWAY

How Do a Pulley and a Wheel and Axle Help Us Do Work?

In this lesson, you can . . .

INVESTIGATE how pulleys work.

LEARN ABOUT pulleys and about wheels and axles.

LINK to math, writing, physical education, and technology.

INVESTIGATE

How a Pulley Works

Activity Purpose Have you ever seen someone raise or lower the flag? Together the rope and wheel on the flagpole make up a pulley (PUHL•ee). Like a lever, a pulley can change the direction of a force. Can a pulley change forces in other ways as levers do? In this investigation you'll **compare** forces to find out.

Materials
- 2 broom handles
- strong rope, 6 m or longer

CAUTION

Activity Procedure

1. Firmly tie one end of the rope to the center of one of the broom handles. This will be Handle 1.

2. Have two people face each other and stand about 30 cm apart. Have one person hold Handle 1. His or her hands should be about 40 cm apart—20 cm on either side of the rope. Have the other person hold the other broom handle (Handle 2) in the same way. (Picture A)

3. Loop the rope around Handle 2 and back over Handle 1. (Picture B)

◄ A pasta maker includes a simple machine—a wheel and axle. As you turn the crank (the wheel), it turns a post (the axle) inside the machine. Blades connected to the axle cut the pasta to the width you want.

4 Stand behind the person holding Handle 1. Have your partners try to hold the broom handles apart while you slowly pull on the free end of the rope. **CAUTION** Don't let fingers get caught between the handles. **Observe** and **record** what happens.

5 Repeat Steps 3 and 4. This time, loop the rope back around Handles 1 and 2 again. (Picture C) **Observe** and **record** what happens.

6 Add more loops around the broom handles. Again pull on the free end of the rope to try to bring the handles together. **Observe** and **record** what happens.

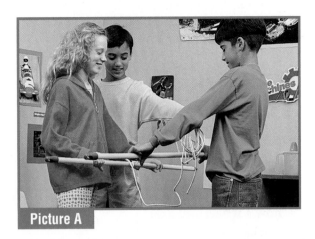
Picture A

Draw Conclusions

1. **Compare** your observations in Steps 4, 5, and 6. Which way of looping the rope made it hardest to pull the handles together? Which way made it easiest?

2. Reread the description of a pulley in the Activity Purpose. What in this investigation worked as wheels do?

3. **Scientists at Work** How did the handles and rope change your effort force? **Compare** this to how levers work. How is it like levers? How is it different?

Picture B

Picture C

Investigate Further How do you think adding loops of rope will change the way the broom handles and rope work? **Form a hypothesis** that explains how adding rope loops will change your results. **Plan and conduct an experiment** to test your hypothesis. Plan to use a spring scale to measure forces.

Process Skill Tip

Scientists often **compare** a new observation to what they know already. When you compare, you look for ways things are alike and ways they are different.

Machines That Turn

Pulleys

FIND OUT

- what fixed and movable pulleys are
- how a wheel and axle works

VOCABULARY

pulley
wheel and axle

You may have seen the wheels of pulleys on a sailboat or a flagpole. A **pulley** is made up of a rope or chain and a wheel around which the rope fits. When you pull down on one rope end, the wheel turns and the other rope end moves up. A pulley that stays in one place is called a *fixed pulley*. Fixed pulleys are often used to raise and lower something lightweight, such as a flag or a small sail, while you stay on the ground or the deck.

A fixed pulley is like a lever that has its fulcrum in the middle. Both the lever and the pulley change only the direction of the effort force. They do not change the size of the effort force.

A different kind of pulley can change the size of the effort force. This pulley is called a movable pulley because it is free to move up and down. One end of its rope is tied down. The load is hooked to the pulley. Pulling up on the rope makes both the pulley and the load rise.

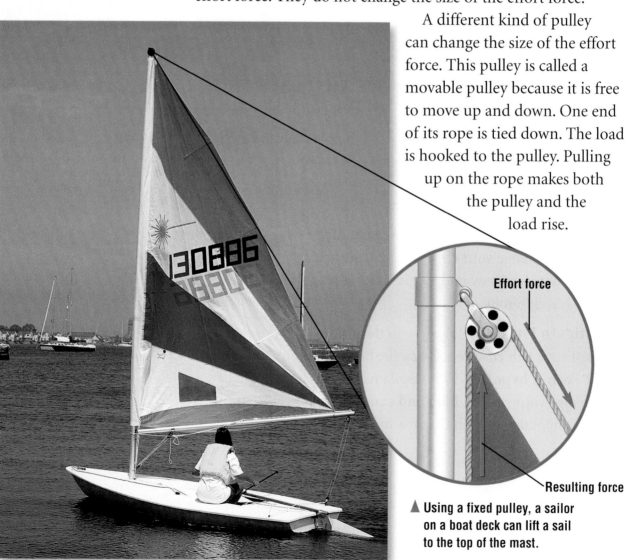

Effort force

Resulting force

▲ Using a fixed pulley, a sailor on a boat deck can lift a sail to the top of the mast.

A movable pulley doesn't change the direction of the effort force. A pull up on the rope also pulls up on the load. But a movable pulley does increase the resulting force. To lift a load of 50 newtons, you need to pull up with only a 25-newton force.

As with a lever, you don't get more work out of a movable pulley than you put in. It doubles your lifting force, but you pull twice as far. To lift a load 2 meters, you must pull up 4 meters of rope.

Pulleys can be put together to make pulley systems, a form of compound machine. For example, you can use a fixed pulley with a movable pulley. The movable pulley increases your force. The fixed pulley changes the direction of your force.

Adding more movable pulleys to a system increases your force even more. Each movable pulley you add also increases the length of rope you must pull to lift a load.

✔ **How does a movable pulley change your force?**

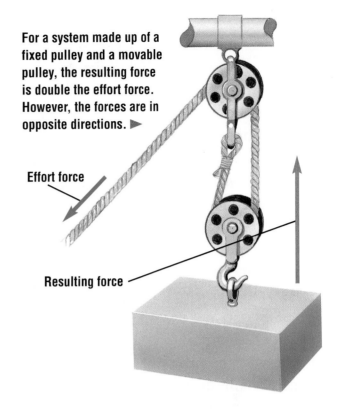

For a system made up of a fixed pulley and a movable pulley, the resulting force is double the effort force. However, the forces are in opposite directions. ▶

Effort force

Resulting force

For a single movable pulley, the resulting force is double the effort force. The resulting and effort forces are in the same direction. ▶

Effort force

Resulting force

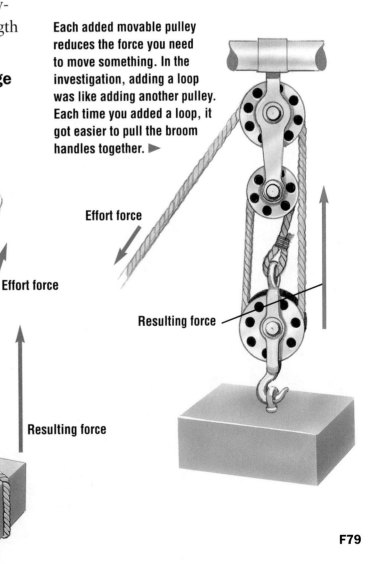

Each added movable pulley reduces the force you need to move something. In the investigation, adding a loop was like adding another pulley. Each time you added a loop, it got easier to pull the broom handles together. ▶

Effort force

Resulting force

Wheels and Axles

A wheel and axle is another simple machine that can make a job easier. A **wheel and axle** (AKS•uhl) is made up of a large wheel attached to a smaller wheel or rod. A doorknob is part of a wheel and axle. The large round knob turns a smaller axle. The axle is what pulls in the latch to open the door. Without the large knob, it would be difficult to turn the axle. The small effort force you use to turn the knob becomes a large resulting force put out by the axle.

As with other simple machines, you can't get more work out of a wheel and axle than you put in. Effort force is made larger. But the distance the outside of the knob turns is larger than the distance the axle moves.

✔ **How does a wheel and axle make a job easier?**

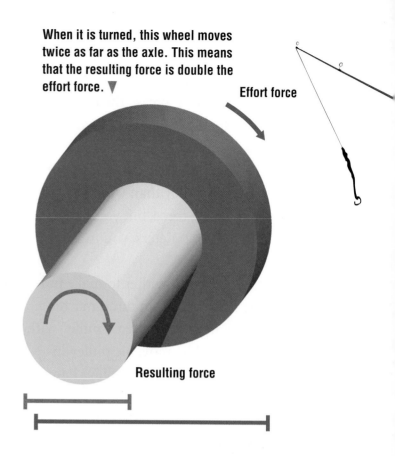

When it is turned, this wheel moves twice as far as the axle. This means that the resulting force is double the effort force. ▼

Effort force

Resulting force

The wheel on this water valve is much larger than the axle. A small effort force on the large wheel makes the axle put out a large resulting force. So the valve is closed tightly but can be opened quickly in an emergency. ▶

Wheel
Axle

FIRE STATION # 4

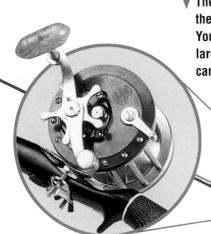

▼ The crank on this fishing reel is the wheel. The reel is the axle. Your effort force becomes a larger resulting force so you can pull in a heavy fish.

Summary

A pulley is a simple machine similar to a lever. A fixed pulley changes the direction of an effort force. A movable pulley makes the resulting force larger than the effort force. Fixed and movable pulleys can be put together to make pulley systems. A wheel and axle is a simple machine in which an effort force on a large wheel makes a larger resulting force on a smaller wheel, or axle.

Review

1. Which kind of pulley makes your effort force larger?
2. Which kind of pulley has the effort force in the opposite direction to the resulting force?
3. Does a wheel and axle change the direction of the effort force, the size of the force, or both? Explain.
4. **Critical Thinking** You want to lift a heavy box 20 meters off the ground. Describe a pulley system that could help you move the box.
5. **Test Prep** Which simple machine can **NOT** be used to increase force?
   - A wheel and axle
   - B lever
   - C fixed pulley
   - D movable pulley

LINKS

MATH LINK

Find a Rule Measure the effort force and resulting force arrows of the pulleys on pages F78–F79. Then look carefully at the pulleys and ropes. Can you find a rule you could use to predict how a pulley or pulley system multiplies your effort force?

WRITING LINK

Persuasive Writing—Opinion Brunel's Portsmouth Pulley Works opened in 1803. It made a pulley called a block and tackle. Suppose you write advertising for this business. Find out more about a block and tackle. Then write a flyer describing the benefits of using pulleys. Explain why the Brunel block and tackle is better than handmade pulleys.

PHYSICAL EDUCATION LINK

Complex Machine A bicycle is a complex machine—a machine made up of two or more compound machines. Observe a bicycle and list all the machines you can find. For each machine, explain how it connects to other machines, or how it makes riding easier or safer for the bicyclist. Make and label a drawing to show what you learned.

TECHNOLOGY LINK

Learn more about amazingly small machines by viewing *Micromachines* on the **Harcourt Science Newsroom Video.**

How Do Some Other Simple Machines Help Us Do Work?

In this lesson, you can . . .

INVESTIGATE an Archimedes' screw.

LEARN ABOUT how inclined planes, screws, and wedges do work.

LINK to math, writing, technology, and other areas.

INVESTIGATE

Make an Archimedes' Screw

Activity Purpose Archimedes (ar•kuh•MEE•deez) was one of the first known scientists. He lived and worked in Greece around 250 B.C. He used science that he learned to make many inventions. One of his inventions, called the Archimedes' screw, is still used all over the world. It is a machine for lifting water. An Archimedes' screw moves water from rivers into canals for irrigation. In this investigation you will **make a model** of an Archimedes' screw and demonstrate how it works.

Materials

- round wooden pole, such as a piece of a broom handle, 20 cm long with nail
- meterstick or metric ruler
- marker
- length of rubber or plastic hose, about 40–50 cm long
- 6 strong rubber bands
- large pan of water or sink that can be filled with water

Activity Procedure

1. Use the meterstick and marker to divide the pole into five equal sections.

2. Use a rubber band to hold the hose to one end of the pole. The band should not be so tight that it closes off the hose, but it should be tight enough to hold the hose in place.

◄ This water-skier flies into the air off the end of a ramp, a common kind of inclined plane.

3 Wind the hose around the pole in a spiral so that it passes over your marks. (Picture A) Use a rubber band to hold the top of the hose in place. Put two or three more bands around the hose and pole so that nothing slips. Wiggle the hose around so the ends open at right angles to the length of the pole. You have built an Archimedes' screw.

4 Put the nail end of the Archimedes' screw in the large pan or sink of water so the device rests on the head of the nail and makes a low angle with the bottom of the pan. Make sure both ends of the screw are over the pan. (Picture B) Turn the Archimedes' screw clockwise 12 times. Now turn the screw in the other direction 12 times. **Observe** what happens.

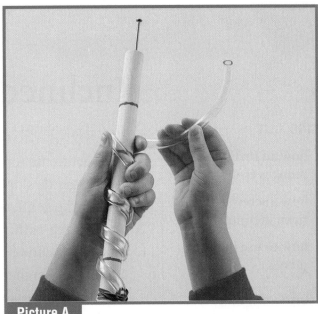
Picture A

Picture B

Draw Conclusions

1. What happened when you turned the Archimedes' screw the first time? What happened the second time?

2. A screw is a type of inclined plane, a flat sloping surface. A ramp is an example of an inclined plane. Where was the inclined plane in the model you made?

3. **Scientists at Work** The Archimedes' screw you built is not a completely useful tool. The screw is hard to turn, and there are easier ways to move water. But it is useful as a **model.** It shows how the machine works. Why might it help to make a small model before building a full-sized machine?

Investigate Further There are many inclined planes around you. Select one day to see how many ramps and screws you can find at school and at home. Make a list of those you find. Tell how each helps people do work.

Process Skill Tip

Scientists often find it helpful to make a small **model** to study an idea or device. Then they can use what they learn from the small model to build a larger device.

Inclined-Plane Machines

Inclined Planes

To get to the top of a mountain, would you rather bicycle along a gentle slope or a steep path? You have to travel much farther on the gentle slope, but you have to use more force to pedal up the steep path. Both slopes are a kind of simple machine called an inclined plane. An **inclined plane** is a flat surface that has one end higher than the other.

An inclined plane changes an effort force into a larger resulting force. The direction of the effort force is along the plane. The resulting force pushes up on the object. When you slide a box up a ramp, you push along the ramp. The ramp pushes up on the box. The steeper the ramp, the less it changes the effort force, and the harder it is to slide the box.

As with other simple machines, you can't get more work from an inclined plane than you put into it. Remember, work is force times distance. An inclined plane is longer than it is high. The distance an object moves along the plane is more than the distance it moves up. So, even though it takes less force to move an object, you have to push it farther.

✓ **How does an inclined plane help you do work?**

FIND OUT

• how an inclined plane reduces effort

• how a screw is related to an inclined plane

• how to use inclined planes as a wedge

VOCABULARY

inclined plane
efficiency
screw
wedge

◄ An inclined plane, or ramp, reduces the force needed to move the box to the height of the truck bed. Using a wheeled cart reduces friction, which makes the ramp more efficient.

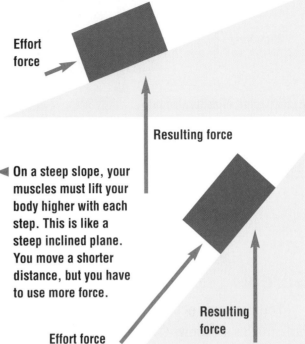

◀ Hiking up a slope that does not rise much for the distance traveled is like going up a gentle inclined plane. You have to travel farther, but you use less force with each step.

Effort force

Resulting force

◀ On a steep slope, your muscles must lift your body higher with each step. This is like a steep inclined plane. You move a shorter distance, but you have to use more force.

Resulting force

Effort force

Efficiency

You actually get less work you can use from an inclined plane than you put into it. When you slide a box up a ramp, some work must go to overcoming friction. That "extra" work does not go into lifting the box. So, an inclined plane is not perfectly efficient. **Efficiency** (eh•FISH•unh•see) is how well a machine changes effort into useful work.

Efficiencies are usually given as percents. An efficiency of 100 percent would be perfect. However, all machines have some friction. So, no machine ever has an efficiency of 100 percent. Most are much lower. For example, most car engines have an efficiency of about 30 percent.

✓ **How does friction affect use of an inclined plane?**

This ramp is an inclined plane. People in wheelchairs can use the ramp instead of stairs. Wheelchair ramps are usually very gentle slopes. This reduces the amount of force needed to move a wheelchair up the ramps. ▼

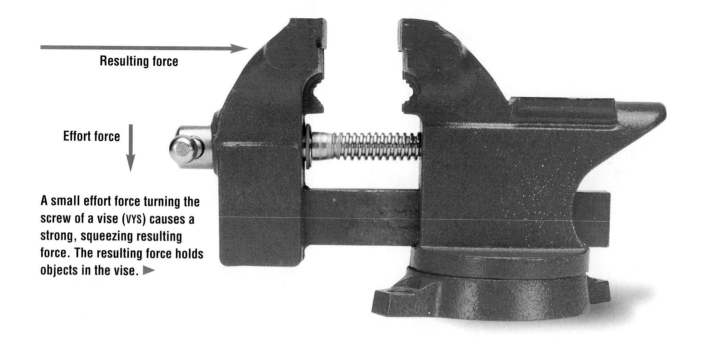

Resulting force

Effort force

A small effort force turning the screw of a vise (VYS) causes a strong, squeezing resulting force. The resulting force holds objects in the vise. ▶

Screws

Wrapping an inclined plane around a pole makes a **screw**. On a screw the long ramp of the inclined plane is wrapped into a space that is the same height as the inclined plane but has almost no width.

Turning a screw moves things up the spiral ramp. The Archimedes' screw you made in the investigation worked this way. Turning the Archimedes' screw pushed water to the top of its tube. The force needed to turn the screw was smaller than the force needed to lift the water straight up.

As other inclined planes do, a screw trades force for distance. The path of the water through the Archimedes' screw was longer than the height it moved up. Lifting the water with an Archimedes' screw used less force.

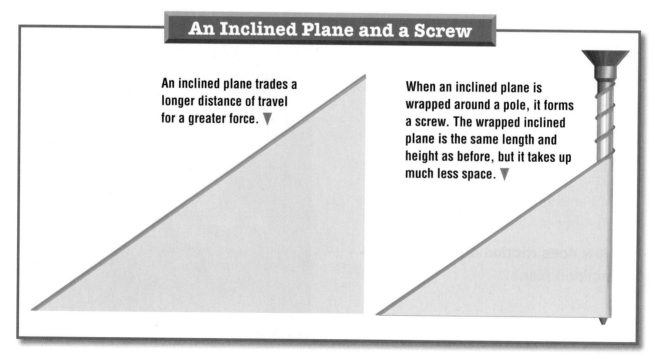

An Inclined Plane and a Screw

An inclined plane trades a longer distance of travel for a greater force. ▼

When an inclined plane is wrapped around a pole, it forms a screw. The wrapped inclined plane is the same length and height as before, but it takes up much less space. ▼

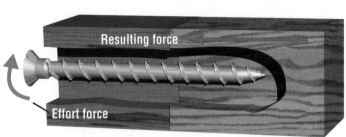

▲ This picture shows wood cut away around a screw. A small effort force turning the screw makes a large resulting force holding the wood pieces together. Also, notice how the wood touches the screw over a large area.

You have probably seen screws holding together pieces of wood or metal. Using screws in this way actually takes several simple machines. The screwdriver used to turn the screw is a wheel and axle. If you start to use a screw by pushing it into the wood, the point of the screw is acting as a wedge.

Why is using a screw better than hammering a nail? A screw takes longer to move into wood. But putting a screw into wood takes less force than putting in a nail. A nail is held in just by friction against the wood. The ridges of a screw hook and hold the wood more tightly.

✔ **How is a screw like an inclined plane?**

Holes are often dug with a kind of screw called an auger (AW•ger). The screw turns to lift dirt up and out of the ground. ▶

◀ A spiral staircase is a form of screw that makes it easier to climb from one floor to another. One advantage of a spiral staircase is that it takes up less space than a regular staircase.

Wedges

Two inclined planes placed back-to-back form a **wedge**. The main difference between a wedge and an inclined plane is how they are used. An inclined plane lifts objects. A wedge pushes things apart. An effort force down on the wide end of a wedge is changed to a much larger resulting force out from the sides of the wedge. Most blades of cutting tools such as knives, chisels, and axes are wedges. Often wedges are combined with levers to make cutting even easier.

✔ **How is a wedge related to an inclined plane?**

▲ The sharp edge of a cooking knife is a wedge. To chop vegetables, a cook may rest the point end of the knife on the cutting board. This makes the knife a compound machine, a combination of a wedge and a lever.

Effort force

Resulting force

Resulting force

As the point of a wedge moves into a solid, the inclined planes of its sides push out. A small effort force on the wide end of the wedge is changed into a much larger resulting force out from its sides. ▶

The blade of an ax is one form of a wedge. The force of the ax down is changed into a resulting force out to the sides that splits the wood. Although chain saws are now used to cut down trees, people still use axes to split wood for fireplaces and stoves. ▶

Summary

An inclined plane is a simple machine used to move things to a different height. It takes more force to move an object up a steep inclined plane than a gently sloping one. When an inclined plane is wrapped around a pole, it becomes a screw. Two inclined planes put together form a wedge.

Review

1. How are screws and wedges related to inclined planes?

2. Name three ways screws are used.

3. Does a screw change the size of the effort force, the direction of the force, or both?

4. **Critical Thinking** How can an inclined plane help you safely lower a heavy object?

5. **Test Prep** Which simple machine is the part of scissors that pushes things apart?

   A screw

   B inclined plane

   C lever

   D wedge

 LINKS

 MATH LINK

Measure Length Measure and compare the effort and resulting force arrows on the top inclined plane on page F85. How many times does the inclined plane multiply your effort force?

 WRITING LINK

Narrative Writing—Story Suppose you must move a piano into a second-floor apartment. Write a short story for your family, describing how you would use simple machines to meet your goal.

 ART LINK

A Museum and a Machine There is a famous inclined plane in the Guggenheim Museum in New York City. Find out its location and its use.

 PHYSICAL EDUCATION LINK

Playing on the Planes Many sports are based on moving up or down an inclined plane. Make a list of sports that use this idea. (HINT: Look at the picture on page F82 to get started.)

  TECHNOLOGY LINK

Visit the Harcourt Learning Site for related links, activities, and resources.

www.harcourtschool.com

Simple Machines and Water Transportation

Since ancient times, people have used boats to explore new areas, to ship goods from one place to another, and just to enjoy traveling. All of the early boats were moved by human muscle and a lever, either a paddle or an oar.

Floating Logs

The earliest boats were probably hollowed-out logs or rafts made of logs tied together with tree roots. Native American peoples made very fine canoes from wood, leather, and tree bark. Dugouts were another type of log boat. A large tree trunk was hollowed out by using fire, a pounding tool called a mallet, and an adz, a simple type of wedge.

Inuits use small hunting boats called kayaks (KY•aks). Kayakers use an unusual oar. It has a paddle blade at each end. This means that the fulcrum of the oar is first at one hand and then at the other as the kayaker puts one end of the oar and then the other in the water.

More Power

The Phoenicians (fuh•NEE•shuhnz) lived on the eastern coast of the Mediterranean Sea. They designed and built ships that were fast because the ships used large teams of rowers. Each side of a ship had one, two, or three long lines of rowers. Each rower had one long oar. The fulcrum of the oar was the point at which the oar went outside the ship.

Looking for ways to make boats faster, boat builders turned to the wind as a source of power. The Egyptians were among the

The History of Water Transportation

Egyptians 3000 B.C.
Egyptians discover use of sails and learn to build ships using wooden planks.

Fulton 1807
Robert Fulton builds the first successful steamship.

3000 B.C. — A.D. 1400 — A.D. 1500 — A.D. 1600 — A.D. 1700 — A.D. 1800

Trireme 500 B.C.
Greeks build ships with sails and three lines of rowers.

Propellers 1836
Propellers to drive steamboats given patent.

Early to mid 1800s

first to build boats that could use either sails or human rowers.

The largest and fastest sailing ships ever made were built in the mid-1800s. They were called clipper ships because they seemed to "clip off" the miles by going so fast. The large sails of a clipper ship were raised using human muscle and a pulley system called a block and tackle. Another simple machine used on clipper ships was a windlass, a type of wheel and axle. With it, a team of people could raise and lower the heavy anchor.

A Lot More Power

During the early 1800s, steam engines changed ship designs forever. Sails slowly disappeared. Newer ships were pushed by huge paddle wheels. Some had a wheel on each side, while others had a single wheel in the back.

In the late 1800s, ships slowly changed from using paddle wheels to using propellers. A propeller looks something like a fan blade. Because of their spiral shape, propellers are sometimes called screws. As a propeller turns, it pulls a boat through the water much as a screw pulls two pieces of wood together. But it takes very big screws

to move a ship. Each of the four propellers on the *Queen Mary*, a British ocean ship launched in 1934, was more than 5 meters (18 ft) across and weighed 38.5 tons!

Today 95 percent of business goods still travel from country to country on the ocean. The power source for large boats has changed from human muscles, to wind, to steam, and finally to other fuels. But simple machines are still on board as part of bigger, more complicated machines.

THINK ABOUT IT

1. Describe two ways simple machines helped to solve problems on a boat or ship.
2. How have more recent ship builders used what earlier people had learned about building boats and ships?

This kayaker's oar is a lever. As he paddles, the fulcrum changes from hand to hand with each stroke.

Today
Huge supercargo ships carry goods all over the world.

A.D. 1900   A.D. 2000

Queen Mary 1934

F91

Wilbur and Orville Wright

INVENTORS

Even as boys, the Wright brothers were fascinated by machines. They sold homemade mechanical toys to earn money when they were young. Orville Wright built his own printing press, and they published a weekly newspaper in Dayton, Ohio. Wilbur Wright was the editor. Later, they began to sell and to rent bicycles. Then they made bicycles in a room above the shop.

The Wright brothers became interested in flying in the 1890s. They read everything they could about how things fly. In 1899 they built their first glider.

In 1903 the two brothers built a biplane, an airplane with two levels of wings. The wings were made by covering wooden frames with cloth and then varnishing the cloth. The two wooden propellers were turned by a 12-horsepower gasoline engine built by the Wrights.

The brothers also made a way to control the plane. A "cradle" was connected to the wings by wires and pulleys. By shifting weight from side to side, the pilot could twist a wing tip to keep the plane balanced.

Orville Wright made the first successful flight on December 17, 1903. He launched the plane from an 18-meter (60-ft) rail on a sand flat. The plane stayed in the air about 12 seconds and flew at about 48 km/hr (30 mi/hr) for just 37 meters (120 ft). The brothers made three more trials that day. Wilbur stayed up the longest—59 seconds—and traveled 260 meters (852 ft).

The brothers preferred to work with no outside help. They improved their airplanes over the next two years. In 1908, Wilbur Wright made the first official public flights in France. The brothers predicted planes would deliver mail and carry passengers. They also hoped that airplanes might prevent a war.

THINK ABOUT IT

1. How do you think the Wrights' work with toys and bicycles prepared them to build a glider?

2. The Wright brothers worked by themselves as a team. What are some benefits of doing that? What are some problems it can cause?

▼ Wilbur Orville ▼

◀ **Wright brothers' biplane at sand flat**

MAKE A SCREW

How are screws and inclined planes related?

Materials

- ruler
- sheet of paper
- scissors
- unsharpened pencil
- tape

Procedure

❶ Draw a right triangle on the paper and cut it out. Imagine that this triangle is an inclined plane.

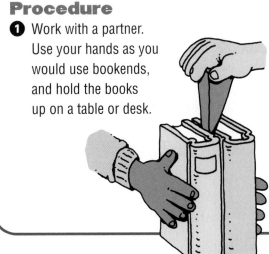

❷ Draw a dark line along the longest edge of the triangle.

❸ Tape the pencil to the back of the inclined plane.

❹ Wrap the triangle around the pencil. Observe the results.

Draw Conclusions

What simple machine have you modeled? How do you know that you could move up the machine and get to the top of the pencil, just as you could move up a straight inclined plane?

USING A WEDGE

How does a wedge work?

Materials

- wooden doorstop
- several books

Procedure

❶ Work with a partner. Use your hands as you would use bookends, and hold the books up on a table or desk.

❷ Have a partner put the narrow end of the doorstop between two of the books and gently push down.

❸ Observe what happens to the books. Record your observations, including how the books felt as your partner pushed down on the doorstop.

❹ Trade roles and repeat the activity.

Draw Conclusions

What did you feel as the doorstop was pushed down? What was the result of the action? What do you think will happen with a wider wedge? A narrower wedge? Try it and see.

Vocabulary Review

Use the terms below to complete the sentences. The page numbers in ( ) tell you where to look in the chapter if you need help.

simple machine (F70)   **wheel and axle** (F80)

lever (F70)   **inclined plane** (F84)

fulcrum (F70)   **efficiency** (F85)

effort force (F70)   **screw** (F86)

work (F74)   **wedge** (F88)

pulley (F78)

1. A basic device that can change the amount or the direction of force, or both at once, is a ____.

2. ____ results when a force produces a movement in the direction of the force.

3. Two inclined planes placed back-to-back form a ____.

4. A simple machine made up of a bar and a fulcrum is a ____.

5. A ____ is made up of an inclined plane wrapped around a pole.

6. To raise a heavy load, you could use a system made up of one fixed ____ and several movable ones.

7. The part of a lever around which the bar moves is the ____.

8. A large wheel connected to a smaller wheel is a ____.

9. ____ is the force that is put into a simple machine.

10. A flat surface that has one end higher than the other is an ____.

11. ____ is how well a machine changes effort into useful force.

Connect Concepts

Use the Venn diagram below to classify the listed machines as either levers or inclined planes.

lever   **screw**   **pulley**   **scissors**

inclined plane   **wedge**   **wheel and axle**   **knife**

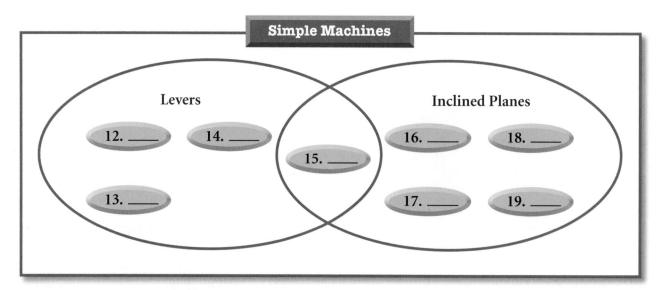

Check Understanding

Write the letter of the best choice.

20. In a lever, the force that is used to move the bar is called the —

A effort force

B resulting force

C fulcrum

D machine

21. When the resulting end of a lever moves a shorter distance than the effort end, it moves with —

F the same force

G no force

H a smaller force

J a greater force

22. To use a pulley to change both force and direction, you need —

A one fixed pulley

B one movable pulley

C one fixed and one movable pulley

D two fixed pulleys

23. When you turn a doorknob, you are using —

F a wheel and axle

G a pulley

H a fulcrum

J an inclined plane

24. A wedge changes an effort force —

A down to a resulting force up

B around to a resulting force straight

C down to a resulting force sideways

D out to a resulting force in

Critical Thinking

For items 25 through 27, describe how you might use each of the following simple machines to remove a large rock from a garden plot. Tell the advantages and disadvantages of using each machine.

25. A lever

26. A pulley (or pulley system)

27. An inclined plane

Process Skills Review

28. You want to calculate the amount of work done as you move a box up a ramp. What do you need to **measure** in order to make your calculations? What tools would be useful in making these measurements?

29. You are digging and making an old-fashioned well. Decide whether to put a fixed pulley or a wheel and axle at the top of the well to raise the bucket. **Compare** these two machines. Explain which you would choose and why.

30. How could you be sure the choice you made in item 29 above is the best one without building the well?

Performance Assessment

Distance and Force

Investigate how the length of a ramp affects the force needed to move a load. Use three boards of different lengths, three books, a spring scale, and a rock. Make a table to record your data. When you have finished, make a bar graph of your data. Use it to explain what you found.

UNIT F EXPEDITIONS

There are many places where you can learn about forces and motion. Visit the places below and learn how electricity is generated and how machines work. You'll also have fun while you learn.

Museum of Science

WHAT A museum featuring science and technology exhibits

WHERE Boston, Massachusetts

WHAT CAN YOU DO THERE? Tour the museum and learn about electricity at the Theater of Electricity exhibit.

The Tech Museum of Innovation

WHAT A hands-on technology museum that works to encourage new ideas

WHERE San Jose, California

WHAT CAN YOU DO THERE? Explore the museum, visit the exhibits, and learn about robots and other machines.

Self-reliant
AUVs

GO ONLINE Plan Your Own Expeditions

If you can't visit the Museum of Science or The Tech Museum of Innovation, visit a museum or a science center near you. Or log on to The Learning Site at **www.harcourtschool.com** to visit these science sites and learn about electricity and machines.

References

Science Handbook

Using Science Tools   **R2**

Using a Hand Lens   R2

Using a Thermometer   R2

Caring for and Using a Microscope   R3

Using a Balance   R4

Using a Spring Scale   R4

Measuring Liquids   R5

Using a Ruler or Meterstick   R5

Using a Timing Device   R5

Glossary   R6

Index   R16

Using Science Tools

Using a Hand Lens

A hand lens magnifies objects, or makes them look larger than they are.

1. Hold the hand lens about 12 centimeters (5 in.) from your eye.

2. Bring the object toward you until it comes into focus.

Using a Thermometer

A thermometer measures the temperature of air and most liquids.

1. Place the thermometer in the liquid. Don't touch the thermometer any more than you need to. Never stir the liquid with the thermometer. If you are measuring the temperature of the air, make sure that the thermometer is not in line with a direct light source.

2. Move so that your eyes are even with the liquid in the thermometer.

3. If you are measuring a material that is not being heated or cooled, wait about two minutes for the reading to become stable, or stay the same. Find the scale line that meets the top of the liquid in the thermometer, and read the temperature.

4. If the material you are measuring is being heated or cooled, you will not be able to wait before taking your measurements. Measure as quickly as you can.

Caring for and Using a Microscope

A microscope is another tool that magnifies objects. A microscope can increase the detail you see by increasing the number of times an object is magnified.

Caring for a Microscope

- Always use two hands when you carry a microscope.
- Never touch any of the lenses of a microscope with your fingers.

Using a Microscope

1. Raise the eyepiece as far as you can by using the coarse-adjustment knob. Place your slide on the stage.

2. Always start by using the lowest power. The lowest-power lens is usually the shortest. Start with the lens in the lowest position it can go without touching the slide.

3. Look through the eyepiece, and begin adjusting it upward with the coarse-adjustment knob. When the slide is close to being in focus, use the fine-adjustment knob.

4. When you want to use a higher-power lens, first focus the slide under low power. Then, watching carefully to make sure that the lens will not hit the slide, turn the higher-power lens into place. Use only the fine-adjustment knob when looking through the higher-power lens.

You may use a Brock microscope. This is a sturdy microscope that has only one lens.

1. Place the object to be viewed on the stage.

2. Look through the eyepiece, and begin raising the tube until the object comes into focus.

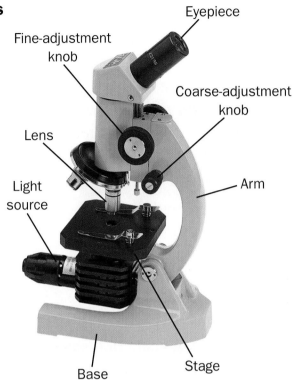

Eyepiece

Fine-adjustment knob

Coarse-adjustment knob

Lens

Light source

Arm

Base

Stage

A Light Microscope

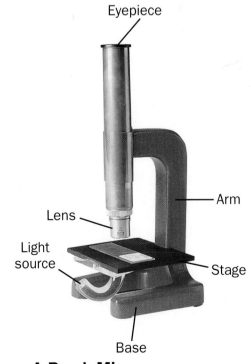

Eyepiece

Arm

Lens

Light source

Stage

Base

A Brock Microscope

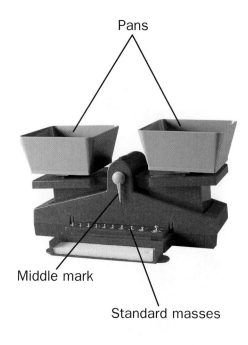

Pans

Middle mark

Standard masses

Using a Balance

Use a balance to measure an object's mass. Mass is the amount of matter an object has.

1. Look at the pointer on the base to make sure the empty pans are balanced.

2. Place the object you wish to measure in the left-hand pan.

3. Add the standard masses to the other pan. As you add masses, you should see the pointer move. When the pointer is at the middle mark, the pans are balanced.

4. Add the numbers on the masses you used. The total is the mass in grams of the object you measured.

Using a Spring Scale

Use a spring scale to measure forces such as the pull of gravity on objects. You measure weight and other forces in units called newtons (N).

Measuring the Weight of an Object

1. Hook the spring scale to the object.

2. Lift the scale and object with a smooth motion. Do not jerk them upward.

3. Wait until any motion of the spring comes to a stop. Then read the number of newtons from the scale.

Measuring the Force to Move an Object

1. With the object resting on a table, hook the spring scale to it.

2. Pull the object smoothly across the table. Do not jerk the object.

3. As you pull, read the number of newtons you are using to pull the object.

Measuring Liquids

Use a beaker, a measuring cup, or a graduate to measure liquids accurately.

1. Pour the liquid you want to measure into a measuring container. Put your measuring container on a flat surface, with the measuring scale facing you.

2. Look at the liquid through the container. Move so that your eyes are even with the surface of the liquid in the container.

3. To read the volume of the liquid, find the scale line that is even with the surface of the liquid.

4. If the surface of the liquid is not exactly even with a line, estimate the volume of the liquid. Decide which line the liquid is closer to, and use that number.

Beaker   **Graduate**

Using a Ruler or Meterstick

Use a ruler or meterstick to measure distances and to find lengths of objects.

1. Place the zero mark or end of the ruler or meterstick next to one end of the distance or object you want to measure.

2. On the ruler or meterstick, find the place next to the other end of the distance or object.

3. Look at the scale on the ruler or meterstick. This will show the distance you want or the length of the object.

Using a Timing Device

Use a timing device such as a stopwatch to measure time.

1. Reset the stopwatch to zero.

2. When you are ready to begin timing, press *Start*.

3. As soon as you are ready to stop timing, press *Stop*.

4. The numbers on the dial or display show how many minutes, seconds, and parts of seconds have passed.

Glossary

As you read your science book, you will see words that may be new to you. The words have phonetic respellings to help you quickly know how to say them. In this Glossary you will see a different kind of respelling. Here, diacritical marks are used, as they are used in dictionaries. *Diacritical respellings* can show more exactly how words should sound.

When you see the ′ mark after a syllable, say that syllable more strongly than the other syllables. The page number after the meaning tells where to find the word in your book. The boldfaced letters in the Pronunciation Key show how each respelling symbol sounds.

PRONUNCIATION KEY

a	**a**dd, m**a**p	m	**m**ove, see**m**	u	**u**p, d**o**ne		
ā	**a**ce, r**a**te	n	**n**ice, ti**n**	û(r)	b**ur**n, t**er**m		
â(r)	**c**are, **air**	ng	ri**ng**, so**ng**	yo͞o	**f**use, **few**		
ä	p**a**lm, f**a**ther	o	**o**dd, h**o**t	v	**v**ain, e**v**e		
b	**b**at, ru**b**	ō	**o**pen, s**o**	w	**w**in, a**w**ay		
ch	**ch**eck, cat**ch**	ô	**o**rder, j**a**w	y	**y**et, **y**earn		
d	**d**og, ro**d**	oi	**oi**l, b**oy**	z	**z**est, mu**s**e		
e	**e**nd, p**e**t	ou	p**ou**t, n**ow**	zh	vi**s**ion, plea**s**ure		
ē	**e**qual, tr**ee**	o͝o	t**oo**k, f**u**ll	ə	the schwa, an		
f	**f**it, hal**f**	o͞o	p**oo**l, f**oo**d		unstressed vowel		
g	**g**o, lo**g**	p	**p**it, sto**p**		representing the sound		
h	**h**ope, **h**ate	r	**r**un, poo**r**		spelled		
i	**i**t, g**i**ve	s	**s**ee, pa**ss**		*a* in **a**bove		
ī	**i**ce, wr**i**te	sh	**s**ure, ru**sh**		*e* in sick**e**n		
j	**j**oy, le**dg**e	t	**t**alk, si**t**		*i* in poss**i**ble		
k	**c**ool, ta**k**e	th	**th**in, bo**th**		*o* in mel**o**n		
l	**l**ook, ru**l**e	t͟h	**th**is, ba**th**e		*u* in circ**u**s		

Other symbols:

• separates words into syllables
′ indicates heavier stress on a syllable
′ indicates light stress on a syllable

A

absorption [ab•sôrp′shən] The stopping of light when it hits a wall or other opaque object **(E106)**

abyssal plains [ə•bis′əl plānz′] Huge flat areas of ocean floor that are covered with thick layers of sediment **(D50)**

acceleration [ak•sel′ər•ā′shən] A change in the speed or direction of an object's motion **(F48)**

adaptation [ad′əp•tā′shən] A body part or behavior that helps an organism meet its needs in its environment **(A48)**

air mass [âr′mas′] A huge body of air which all has similar temperature and moisture **(D13)**

air pressure [âr′presh′ər] Particles of air pressing down on the Earth's surface **(D7)**

amplitude [am′plə•tōōd′] A measure of the strength of a sound wave; shown by height on a wave diagram **(E72)**

anthracite [an′thrə•sīt′] A hard, black rock; fourth stage of coal formation **(C55)**

artery [är′tər•ē] A blood vessel that carries blood away from the heart **(A105)**

arthropod [är′thrə•pod] An invertebrate with legs that have several joints **(A16)**

asteroid [as′tə•roid] A small rocky object that moves around the sun **(D71)**

atmosphere [at′məs•fir] The layer of air that surrounds our planet **(D6)**

axis [ak′sis] An imaginary line which runs through both poles of a planet **(D65)**

B

barometer [bə•rom′ət•ər] An instrument that measures air pressure **(D20)**

bituminous coal [bī•tōō′mə•nəs kōl′] A fairly hard, dark brown or black rock; third stage of coal formation **(C55)**

brain [brān] The control center of your nervous system **(A110)**

buoyancy [boi′ən•sē] The ability of matter to float in a liquid or gas **(E20)**

C

camouflage [kam′ə•fläzh′] An animal's color or pattern that helps it blend in with its surroundings **(A52)**

capillary [kap′ə•ler′ē] A tiny blood vessel that allows gases and nutrients to pass from blood to cells **(A104)**

carbon dioxide [kär′bən dī•ok′sīd′] A gas breathed out by animals **(A72)**

cardiac muscle [kär′dē•ak mus′əl] A type of muscle that works the heart **(A99)**

cast [kast] A fossil formed when sediments or minerals fill a mold; it takes on the same outside shape as the living thing that shaped the mold **(C38)**

cell [sel] The basic building block of life **(A6)**

cell membrane [sel′ mem′brān] The thin layer that encloses and gives shape to a cell **(A7)**

cell wall [sel′ wôl′] A structure that keeps a cell rigid and provides support to an entire plant **(A8)**

charge [chärj] A measure of the extra positive or negative particles that an object has **(F6)**

chemical change [kem′i•kəl chānj′] A change that produces one or more new substances and may release energy **(E28)**

chemical reaction [kem′i•kəl rē•ak′shən] Another term for chemical change **(E28)**

chloroplast [klôr′ə•plast′] A part of a plant cell that contains chlorophyll, the green pigment plants need to make their food **(A8)**

circuit [sûr′kit] A path that is made for an electric current **(F12)**

cirrus [sir′əs] Wispy, high-altitude clouds that are made up of ice crystals **(D15)**

climate [klī′mit] The average temperature and rainfall of an area over many years **(A41, B28)**

comet [kom′it] A small mass of dust and ice that orbits the sun in a long, oval-shaped path **(D71)**

community [kə•myoo′nə•tē] All the populations that live in the same area **(B14)**

compression [kəm•presh′ən] The part of a sound wave in which air is pushed together **(E71)**

condensation [kon′dən•sā′shən] The process by which water vapor changes from a gas to liquid **(D34)**

conduction [kən•duk′shən] The transfer of thermal energy caused by particles of matter bumping into each other **(E49)**

conductor [kən•duk′tər] A material that electric current can pass through easily **(F13)**

conservation [kon′sər•vā′shən] The careful management and wise use of natural resources **(B68)**

consumer [kən•soo′mər] A living thing that eats other living things for energy **(B21)**

continental shelf [kon′tə•nen′təl shelf′] The ocean floor of the shore zone **(D49)**

convection [kən•vek′shən] The transfer of thermal energy by particles of a liquid or gas moving from one place to another **(E50)**

core [kôr] The dense center of Earth; a ball made mostly of two metals, iron and nickel **(C6)**

crater [krā′tər] A large basin formed at the top of a volcano when the top falls in on itself **(C22)**

crust [krust] Earth's outer layer; includes the rock of the ocean floor and large areas of land **(C6)**

cumulonimbus [kyoo′myoo•lō•nim′bəs] Towering, dark rain clouds with a nimbus, or halo, of gray-white **(D15)**

cumulus [kyoom′yə•ləs] Puffy cotton-ball clouds that begin to form when water droplets condense at middle altitudes **(D15)**

cytoplasm [sīt′ō•plaz′əm] A jellylike substance that fills most of the space in a cell **(A7)**

decomposer [dē′kəm•pōz′ər] A living thing that feeds on the wastes of plants and animals or on their remains after they die **(B21)**

deep ocean current [dēp′ ō′shən kûr′ənt] An

ocean current formed when cold water flows underneath warm water **(D44)**

density [den′sə•tē] The property of matter that compares the amount of matter to the space it takes up **(E14)**

dissolve [di•zolv′] To form a solution with another material **(E19)**

diversity [di•vûr′sə•tē] Variety **(B29)**

dormancy [dôr′mən•sē] State of much lower activity that some plants enter to survive colder weather **(A78)**

earthquake [ûrth′kwāk′] A vibration, or shaking, of Earth's crust **(C14)**

echo [ek′ō] A sound reflection **(E86)**

ecosystem [ek′ō•sis′təm] Groups of living things and the environment they live in **(B12)**

efficiency [i•fish′ən•sē] How well a machine changes effort into useful work **(F85)**

effort force [ef′ərt fôrs′] The force put on one part of a simple machine, for example, when you push or pull on a lever **(F70)**

electric cell [i•lek′trik sel′] A device that supplies energy to move charges through a circuit **(F12)**

electric current [i•lek′trik kûr′ənt] A flow of electric charges **(F12)**

electric field [i•lek′trik fēld′] The space around an object in which electric forces occur **(F8)**

electromagnet [i•lek′trō•mag′nit] An arrangement of wire wrapped around a core, producing a temporary magnet **(F25)**

embryo [em′brē•ō] A young plant **(A20)**

energy [en′ər•jē] The ability to cause a change **(E42)**

energy pyramid [en′ər•jē pir′ə•mid] A diagram that shows how much food energy is passed from one organism to another along a food chain **(B22)**

environment [in•vī′rən•mənt] Everything that surrounds and affects an animal, including living and nonliving things **(A40)**

epicenter [ep′i•sent′ər] The point on the surface of Earth that is right above the focus of an earthquake **(C15)**

esophagus [i•sof′ə•gəs] The tube that connects your mouth with your stomach **(A112)**

evaporation [ē•vap′ə•rā′shən] The process in which a liquid changes to a gas **(D34)**

fault [fôlt] A break in Earth's crust along which rocks move **(C14)**

fibrous roots [fī′brəs rōōts′] Long roots that grow near the surface **(A79)**

flowers [flou′ərz] Reproductive structures in flowering plants **(A22)**

focus [fō′kəs] The point underground where the movement of an earthquake first takes place **(C15)**

food web [fōōd′ web′] A diagram that shows how food chains connect and overlap **(B23)**

force [fôrs] A push or pull **(F46)**

fossil [fos′əl] A preserved clue to life on Earth long ago **(C36)**

fossil fuel [fos′əl fyoo′əl] Fuel formed from the remains of organisms that lived long ago **(C52)**

frame of reference [frām′ uv ref′ər•əns] The things around you that you can sense and use to describe motion **(F41)**

friction [frik′shən] A force that keeps objects that are touching each other from sliding past each other easily **(F58)**

front [frunt] The border where two air masses meet **(D14)**

fruit [froot] The part of a flowering plant that surrounds and protects the seeds **(A22)**

fuel [fyoo′əl] A material that can burn **(E56)**

fulcrum [fool′krəm] The fixed point, or point that doesn't move, on a lever **(F70)**

fungi [fun′jī′] Living things that look like plants but cannot make their own food; for example, mushrooms **(A26)**

gas [gas] The state of matter that has no definite shape and takes up no definite amount of space **(E8)**

gas giants [gas′ jī′ənts] Planets which are large spheres made up mostly of gases—for example, Jupiter, Saturn, Uranus, and Neptune **(D78)**

germinate [jûr′mə•nāt′] To sprout; said of a seed **(A84)**

gravity [grav′ə•tē] A force that pulls all objects toward each other **(F56)**

greenhouse effect [grēn′hous′ i•fekt′] The warming of Earth caused by the atmosphere trapping thermal energy from the sun **(D12)**

habitat [hab′ə•tat′] An environment that meets the needs of an organism **(B20)**

heart [härt] The muscle that pumps blood through blood vessels to all parts of the body **(A105)**

heat [hēt] The transfer of thermal energy from one piece of matter to another **(E48)**

hibernation [hī′bər•nā′shən] A period when an animal goes into a long, deep "sleep" **(A59)**

humidity [hyoo•mid′ə•tē] The amount of water vapor in the air **(D21)**

hygrometer [hī•grom′ə•tər] A tool to measure moisture in the air **(D21)**

hyphae [hī′fē] Densely packed threadlike parts of a fungus **(A27)**

inclined plane [in′klīnd plān′] A flat surface with one end higher than the other **(F84)**

infrared radiation [in′frə•red′ rā′dē•ā′shən] The bundles of light energy that transfer heat **(E52)**

inner planets [in′ər plan′its] The planets closest to the sun; Mercury, Venus, Earth, and Mars **(D76)**

instinct [in′stingkt] A behavior that an animal begins life with **(A56)**

insulator [in′sə•lāt′ər] A material that current cannot pass through easily **(F13)**

intertidal zone [in′tər•tīd′əl zōn′] A narrow strip, along the shore, that is covered with water during high tide and exposed during low tide **(B36)**

invertebrate [in•vûr′tə•brit] An animal without a backbone **(A16)**

kinetic energy [ki•net′ik en′ər•jē] Energy of motion **(E42)**

large intestine [lärj′ in•tes′tən] The last part of the digestive system where water is removed from food **(A113)**

lava [lä′və] Melted rock that reaches Earth's surface **(C20)**

lever [lev′ər] A simple machine made up of a bar that turns on a fixed point **(F70)**

lignite [lig′nīt] A soft, brown rock; the second stage of coal formation **(C55)**

liquid [lik′wid] The state of matter that takes the shape of its container and takes up a definite amount of space **(E7)**

loudness [loud′nes] Your perception of the amount of sound energy reaching your ear **(E78)**

lungs [lungz] The main organs of the respiratory system **(A104)**

magma [mag′mə] Melted rock inside Earth **(C20)**

magma chamber [mag′mə chām′bər] An underground pool that holds magma, below a volcano **(C21)**

magnet [mag′nit] An object that attracts certain materials, such as iron or steel **(F18)**

magnetic field [mag•net′ik fēld′] The space all around a magnet where the force of the magnet can act **(F19)**

magnetic pole [mag•net′ik pōl′] The end of a magnet **(F18)**

mantle [man′təl] The thickest layer of Earth; found just below the crust **(C6)**

mass [mas] The amount of matter something contains **(E6)**

matter [mat′ər] Everything in the universe that has mass and takes up space **(E6)**

metamorphosis [met′ə•môr′fə•sis] The process of change; for example, from an egg to an adult butterfly **(A44)**

microorganisms [mī′krō•ôr′gən•iz′əmz] Organisms that are so small they can only be seen with a microscope; many have only one cell **(A9)**

mid-ocean ridge [mid′ō•shən rij′] A vast chain of mountains that runs along the centers of Earth's oceans **(D50)**

migration [mī•grā′shən] The movement of a group of one type of animal from one region to another and back again **(A57)**

mimicry [mim′ik•rē] An adaptation in which an animal looks very much like another animal or an object **(A52)**

mold [mōld] A common type of fungi that often look cottony or woolly **(A28)**

mold [mōld] A fossil imprint made by the outside of a dead plant or animal **(C38)**

motion [mō′shən] A change of position **(F40)**

natural gas [nach′ər•əl gas′] A gas, mostly methane, usually found with petroleum **(C53)**

near-shore zone [nir′shôr′ zōn′] Ocean zone that starts at the low-tide mark and goes out into the ocean **(B36)**

nerve [nûrv] A group of neurons that carries signals from the brain to the body and from the body to the brain **(A110)**

neuron [noor′on′] A nerve cell **(A110)**

newton [noo′tən] The metric, or Système International (SI), unit of force **(F51)**

niche [nich] The role or part played by an organism in its habitat **(B21)**

nucleus [noo′klē•əs] A cell's control center **(A7)**

nutrient [noo′trē•ənt] A substance, such as a mineral, which all living things need in order to grow **(A72)**

opaque [ō•pāk′] Reflecting or absorbing all light; no image can be seen **(E106)**

open-ocean zones [ō′pən•ō′shən zōnz′] The deep parts of the oceans, located far from shore **(B36)**

orbit [ôr′bit] The path that an object such as a planet makes as it revolves around a second object **(D64)**

organ [ôr′gən] A group of tissues of different kinds working together to perform a task **(A98)**

outer planets [ou′tər plan′its] The planets farthest from the sun; Jupiter, Saturn, Uranus, Neptune, and Pluto **(D78)**

oxygen [ok′si•jən] One of the many gases in air **(A41)**

parallel circuit [par′ə•lel sûr′kit] A circuit that has more than one path along which current can travel **(F14)**

peat [pēt] A soft, brown material made up of partly decayed plants; first stage of coal formation **(C55)**

petroleum [pə•trō′lē•əm] A thick brown or black liquid fossil fuel; crude oil **(C53)**

phase [fāz] One of the different shapes the moon seems to have as it orbits around Earth **(D64)**

photosynthesis [fōt′ō•sin′thə•sis] The process by which a plant makes its own food **(A73)**

physical change [fiz′i•kəl chānj′] Any change in the size, shape, or state of a substance **(E26)**

pistil [pis′təl] A flower part that collects pollen **(A85)**

pitch [pich] A measure of how high or low a sound is **(E79)**

planet [plan′it] A large object that moves around a star **(D71)**

plate [plāt] Continent-sized slab of Earth's crust and upper mantle **(C8)**

pollination [pol′ə•na′shən] Transfer of pollen from a stamen to a pistil by wind or animals **(A85)**

population [pop′yoo•la′shən] A group of the same species living in the same place at the same time **(B13)**

position [pə•zish′ən] A certain place **(F40)**

precipitation [prē•sip′ə•tā′shən] Water that falls to Earth as rain, snow, sleet, or hail **(D35)**

preservation [prez′ər•vā′shən] The protection of an area **(B72)**

prism [priz′əm] A solid object that bends light; not a lens **(E110)**

producer [prə•dōōs′ər] A living thing, such as a plant, that makes its own food **(B21)**

pulley [pŏŏl′ē] A simple machine made up of a rope or chain and a wheel around which the rope or chain fits **(F78)**

radiation [rā′dē•ā′shən] The bundles of energy that move through matter and through empty space **(E52)**

reclamation [rek′lə•mā′shən] The repairing of some of the damage done to an ecosystem **(B63)**

redesign [rē′di•zīn′] Changing the design of packaging or products in order to use fewer resources **(B71)**

reflection [ri•flek′shən] The bouncing of light off an object **(E102)**

refraction [ri•frak′shən] The bending of the path of light when it moves from one kind of matter to another **(E104)**

relative motion [rel′ə•tiv mō′shən] A motion that is described based on a frame of reference **(F41)**

resistor [ri•zis′tər] A material that resists the flow of current but doesn't stop it **(F13)**

revolution [rev′ə•lōō′shən] The movement of any object in an orbit, such as Earth moving around the sun **(D65)**

rotation [rō•tā′shən] The motion of a planet or other object as it turns on its axis **(D65)**

salinity [sə•lin′ə•tē] The amount of salt in water **(B30)**

satellite [sat′ə•līt′] An object that moves around another object in space; the moon is a satellite of Earth **(D64)**

screw [skrōō] An inclined plane wrapped around a pole **(F86)**

seismograph [sīz′mə•graf′] An instrument that records earthquake waves **(C16)**

series circuit [sir′ēz sûr′kit] A circuit that has only one path for current **(F14)**

shelter [shel′tər] A place where an animal is protected from other animals or from the weather **(A43)**

shore zone [shôr′ zōn′] The place where land and ocean meet **(D49)**

simple machine [sim′pəl mə•shēn′] One of the basic machines that make up other machines **(F70)**

small intestine [smôl′ in•tes′tən] A long tube of muscle where most food is digested **(A112)**

smooth muscle [smōōth′ mus′əl] A type of muscle found in the walls of some organs such as the stomach, intestines, blood vessels, and bladder **(A99)**

solar energy [sō′lər en′ər•jē] The energy given off by the sun **(E57)**

solar system [sō′lər sis′təm] A group of objects in space that move around a central star **(D70)**

solid [sol′id] The state of matter that has a definite shape and takes up a definite amount of space **(E6)**

solubility [sol′yōō•bil′ə•tē] A measure of the amount of a material that will dissolve in another material **(E19)**

solution [sə•lōō′shən] A mixture in which the particles of different kinds of matter are mixed evenly with each other and particles do not settle out **(E18)**

sonic boom [son′ik bōōm′] A shock wave of compressed sound waves produced by an object moving faster than sound **(E88)**

sound [sound] A series of vibrations that you can hear **(E70)**

sound wave [sound′ wāv′] A moving pattern of high and low pressure that you can hear **(E71)**

space probe [spās′ prōb′] An uncrewed space vehicle that carries cameras, instruments, and other research tools **(D88)**

speed [spēd] A measure of an object's change in position during a unit of time; for example, 10 meters per second **(F42)**

speed of sound [spēd′ uv sound′] The speed at which a sound wave travels through a given material **(E84)**

spinal cord [spi′nəl kôrd′] The tube of nerves that runs through your spine, or backbone **(A110)**

spore [spôr] A tiny cell that ferns and fungi use to reproduce **(A27, A85)**

stability [stə•bil′ə•tē] The condition that exists when the changes in a system over time cancel each other out **(B8)**

stamen [stā′mən] A flower part that makes pollen **(A85)**

star [stär] A huge, burning sphere of gases; for example, the sun **(D70)**

static electricity [stat′ik ē′lek•tris′i•tē] An electric charge that stays on an object **(F6)**

stomach [stum′ək] A bag made up of smooth muscles that mixes food with digestive juices **(A112)**

storm surge [stôrm′ sûrj′] A very large series of waves caused by high winds over a large area of ocean **(D41)**

stratosphere [strat′ə•sfir′] The layer of atmosphere that contains ozone and is located above the troposphere **(D8)**

stratus [strā′təs] Dark gray clouds that form a low layer and sometimes bring light rain or snow showers **(D15)**

striated muscle [strī′āt•ed mus′əl] A muscle with light and dark stripes; a muscle you can control by thinking **(A100)**

succession [sək•sesh′ən] The process that gradually changes an existing ecosystem into another ecosystem **(B52)**

surface current [sûr′fis kûr′ənt] An ocean current formed when steady winds blow over the surface of the ocean **(D44)**

system [sis′təm] A group of parts that work together as a unit **(B6)**

taproot [tap′rōōt′] A plant's single main root that goes deep into the soil **(A79)**

telescope [tel′ə•skōp′] A device people use to observe distant objects with their eyes **(D84)**

temperature [tem′pər•ə•chər] A measure of the average energy of motion of the particles in matter **(E43)**

thermal energy [thûr′məl en′ər•jē] The energy of the random motion of particles in matter **(E42)**

tide [tīd] The daily changes in the local water level of the ocean **(D42)**

tissue [tish′oo] A group of cells of the same type **(A98)**

trace fossil [trās′ fos′əl] A fossil that shows changes that long-dead animals made in their surroundings **(C37)**

translucent [trans•loo′sənt] Allowing some light to pass through; blurry image can be seen **(E106)**

transparent [trans•pâr′ənt] Allows most light to pass through; clear image can be seen **(E106)**

transpiration [tran′spə•rā′shən] The giving off of water vapor by plants **(A78)**

trenches [trench′əz] Valleys that form on the ocean floor where two plates come together; the deepest places in the oceans **(D50)**

troposphere [trō′pə•sfir′] The layer of atmosphere closest to Earth **(D8)**

tuber [too′bər] A swollen underground stem **(A87)**

vein [vān] A large blood vessel that returns blood to the heart **(A105)**

vent [vent] In a volcano, the rocky opening through which magma rises toward the surface **(C20)**

vertebrate [vûr′tə•brit] An animal with a backbone **(A16)**

visible spectrum [viz′ə•bəl spek′trəm] The range of light energy that people can see **(E110)**

volcano [vol•kā′nō] A mountain that forms when red-hot melted rock flows through a crack onto Earth's surface **(C20)**

volume [vol′yoom] The amount of space that matter takes up **(E13)**

water cycle [wôt′ər sī′kəl] The constant recycling of water on Earth **(D34)**

wave [wāv] An up-and-down movement of water **(D40)**

wavelength [wāv′length] The distance from one compression to the next in a sound wave **(E72)**

wedge [wej] A machine made up of two inclined planes placed back-to-back **(F88)**

weight [wāt] A measure of the force of gravity upon an object **(F57)**

wheel and axle [hwēl′ and ak′səl] A simple machine made up of a large wheel attached to a smaller wheel or rod **(F80)**

work [wûrk] That which is done on an object when a force moves the object through a distance **(F74)**

A

Abdominal muscles, R28
Absorption, E106
Abyssal plains, D50
Acceleration, F48
  pushing and, F49
Activity pyramid, R12
Adams, John C., D91
Adaptations, A48
  animal, A48–53, A56–61
  plant, A74, A80
Agricola, Georgius, C58
Air
  in atmosphere, D6
  property of, D4–5
  sun and, D12
Air masses, D13
  meeting of, D14
  over water, D21
Airplane, inventors of, F92
Air pressure, D7, D18–20
Aldabra tortoises, A37
Aldrin, Edwin, D87
Algae
  in food chain, B21
  green, A4
  as one-celled organisms, A9
  polyps and, B30
Aluminum
  density of, E3
  recycling, B69
American bison, A51
American cockroach, A62
American holly, A22
Ammonoids, C33–34
Amoeba, A9
Ampere, F12
Amplitude, E72–73
Anaconda, B29
Anemometer, D21
Anemone, B31, D42
Animal adaptations
  behaviors, A56–61
  body parts, A48–53
Animal behaviorist, A64
Animal cells, A7
Animals
  body coverings, A50
  body supports, A16
  body types, A14–15

color and shape, A52
  fast, A36
  hibernation of, A59
  largest, A3
  learned behaviors of, A60–61
  migration of, A57
  needs of, A40–45
  tracks, C40
  and their young, A44
  in tropical rain forests, B32
Animal tracks, C40
Animatronic dinosaur, C45
Anthracite, C55
Antiquities Act, B74–75
Ants, A16, A68
  robot, A62–63
Apollo 11, D87
Appalachian Trail, B75
Archaeopteryx, C42
Archer, F46
Archimedes' screw, F82–83
Arctic fox, A43
Arms
  bones and muscles in, A99
  movement, A100
Armstrong, Neil, D87
Arteries, A105–106, R32
Arthropods, A16
Ascension Island, A57
Asteroids, D71
Astronauts, F62
  Apollo mission, D87
  space shuttle, D87
  using moon rover, D82
Atlantic green turtle, A57
Atlantic Ocean, D31
Atlas statue, E3
Atmosphere, D6
  greenhouse effect, D12
  layers of, D8
  mass of 1-m×1-m column, D7
  telescopes and, D85
Atmospheric scientist, D26
Auger, F87
Axis, D65
  Earth's, D72

B

Babbage, Charles, F67
Backbone, A99

Bacteria
  as decomposers, B21
  fighting, R10
  in soil, A2
Balance, using, R4
Barometer, D20
Barrel cactus, A75
Bathyscaph, D54
Bats
  echoes and, E66
  North American, A59
  skeleton of, A17
  sound and hearing of, E67
Bay of Fundy, D42
Beaker, R5
Bears
  brown, A42
  in food chain, B21
  polar, A50
Behaviors
  adaptive, A56–61
  instinctual, A56
  learned, A60–61
Berson, Dr. Solomon, A116
BetaSweet carrots, A88–89
Biceps, A99–100, R28–29
Bicycle
  friction and, F58–59
  helmet, R17
  safety, R16–17
  Ultimate Bike, F61
Bicycle mechanic, F61
Birds
  adaptations, A49
  beaks, A46–48
  carrying seeds, A84
  migration of, A58
Bituminous coal, C55
Black-footed ferrets, B48
Blizzard safety, R19
Blood, A105–107
Blood cells, R33
Blood vessels, R32
Blue jets, D25
Blue-ringed octopus, A12
Blue whale, A3
Boats, F90–91
Bobsled, accelerating, F49
Boiling points (chart), E38
Bones
  dinosaur, C44
  human, A98–99

Botanist, A90
Bracket fungi, A28
Brain, human, A110, R36–37
Brain coral, B31
Bread mold, A28
Breastbone, A99
Breathing, A104–106, R35
   rates, A102–103
Bridges, B3
Bristlecone pine, A69
British soldier lichen, A29
Brock microscope, R3
Bronchi, R35
Brown bears, A42
Bulbs
   light, E39
   tulip, A86
Bullhorn acacia, A68
Bunsen burner, E29
Buoyancy, E20
Buoys, D32
Burning
   as chemical change, E29–30
   fuel, E56
Butterfly
   metamorphosis, A44
   monarch, A54–57
   morpho, B29
   viceroy, A52

C

Cactus
   adaptations of, A74
   barrel, A75
   need for water, A70
   saguaro, A69
Caiman, B29
Calf muscle, A99
California condor, B49
Callisto, D88
Camouflage, A52
Capillaries, A104–105
Capuchin, B29
Capybara, B29
Carbon dioxide, A72
   in atmosphere, D6
   forming a mixture, E29
   greenhouse effect and, E56
   heart, lungs, and, A106–107

   human respiratory system and, A104
   photosynthesis and, A73, D7
   polyps and, B30
Car braking (chart), F37
Cardiac muscle, A99, A100–101
Caribou, B2-3
Carson, Rachel, D56
Cast, fossil, C38
Caterpillar, A44, B25
Cell membrane, A7–8
Cell(s), A6
   animal, A7
   blood, A95, R33
   bone, A98
   model of, A4–5
   plant, A8
   replacement of human, A94
Cell wall, A8
Centipede, A16
Chameleon, A42, A52
Chanterelle, A27
Charge, F6
Chase, Mary Agnes Meara, A90
Cheetah, A36, A60
Chemical changes, E28, E30
Chemical energy, E28
Chemical reaction, E28
Chemicals
   and ecosystem damage, B60
   testing water for, B73
Chimpanzee, A60, A64
Chlorophyll, A73
Chloroplasts, A8
Chrysalis, A44
Cinder cone volcanoes, C21
Circuit, F12
   parallel, F14
   series, F14
Circulatory system, A105, R32-33
Cirrus cloud, D15
Clavicle, R26
Cleaner wrasse, B31
Cliff swallows, B3
Climate, A41, B28
Closterium, A4
Cloud(s)
   formation of, D34
   types, D15
Clownfish, B31

Coal
   burning, E56
   formation of, C54
   types, C55
Cold front, D14–15
Collarbone, A99, R26
Colors
   adding, E112
   basic, E112
   light and, E110–113
   seeing, E112
Colo volcano, C24
Comets, D71
Community, B14
Compass, F30
Composite volcanoes, C21
Compression, E71
Computer models of ecosystems, B42–43
Computer programmer, B43
Computers
   cooling systems for, E59
   first, F67
   safe use, R14
Concave lenses, E115
Condensation, in water cycle, D34
Conduction, E49
Conductor, F13
Cone-bearing plants, A20–21
Cones, A18–19
Conservation, B68
   in national parks, B75
   of resources, B68–73
Consumers, B21
Continental shelf, D49
Continents, C6
Convection, E50
Copper, density of, E3
Coprolites, C37
Coral, B30–31, B64
Coral reef, B26–27
   ecosystem, B30
   map of, B28
   water temperatures in, B30
Core, Earth's, C6–7
Cork tree, A6
Cowles, Dr. Henry Chandler, B44

Crabs, D42
Crater, C22
Crater Lake, OR, C22–23
Craters, moon's, D61, D84
Crewed missions, D87
Crinoid, B31
Crocodile, saltwater, A3
Crust, Earth's, C6–7
Cumulonimbus, D15
Cumulus, D15
Curare, B33
Curveball, F38
Customary measures, R6
Cuvier, Georges, C58–59
Cycad, A20
Cytoplasm
    in animal cells, A7
    in plant cells, A8

Dante, C26–27
Dante II, C26–27
Darwin's finch, A48
Dead Sea, D36
Decomposers, B21, B28
Decorator crab, B31
Deep Flight II, D54–55
Deep-ocean currents, D44
Deimos, D80
Deltoid, A99, R28
Density, E14
    of common materials
    (chart), E3
Deposition, D41
Desert, A40
Desert fox, A43
Dial spring scale, F52
Diaphragm, R34
Diatoms, B31
Digestive system
    in humans, A111–112, R30–31
    in snails, A15
Dinosaurs
    animatronic, C45
    bones of, C36, C44
    duckbill, C58
    footprints of, C33
    fossils of, C32, C40
Diorama, B27

Disease, species endangerment
    and, B48
Dissolve, E19, E27
Diversity, B29
Dodder, A69
Dogs, sound and hearing of, E67
Dolphins
    hair on, A51
    sound and hearing of, E67
    speed of, A36
Dormancy, A78
Drawbridge, F67
Dromaeosaurs, C32
Duckbill dinosaur, C58

Earle, Sylvia, D54
Ears, caring for, R24
Earth
    atmosphere of, D6–9
    axis of, D65
    comparative size of, D70
    distance from moon, D62
    distance from sun, D60, D69
    gravity between sun and, F56
    as inner planet, D76–77
    layers of, C4–5, C7–8
    mass of, E2
    orbit of, D64–65
    planet year of, D72
    revolution of, D65
    rotation of, D65
    seasons and, D66
    structure of, C6–7
    tilt of, D61
    weight on (chart), F57
Earthquake(s), C14
    in California, C14
    destruction from, C12, C28
    epicenter of, C15
    focus of, C15
    measuring, C14–17
    New Madrid, Missouri, C3
    safety, R19
    Tokyo, Japan, C28
Earthworms, A15
Echo, E86
Eastern hemlock, A78
Ecologist, B44

Ecosystem(s), B12
    adding to, B64–65
    change in, B24
    communities in, B14
    computer models of, B42–43
    conservation of, B75
    damage to, B60–61
    forest, B63
    humans and, B60–65
    living parts of, B12
    living things in, B20–25
    populations in, B13
    protected, B72
    rapid changes in, B54–57
    repair of, B62–63
    roles in, B21
    seashore, B43
    tropical, B28–33
    water, B61
    yard as, B10–11
Edison, Thomas A., F31
Efficiency, F85
Effort force
    with inclined plane, F85
    with lever, F70–71, F74
    with pulley, F78–79
    with screw, F86
    with wedges, F88
    with wheel and axle, F80
Eggs, insect, A44
Egrets, B13
Electric
    cell, F12
    current, F12
    field, F8
Electricity
    history of, F30–31
    origin of word, F30
    static, F30
    use (chart), F3
    U.S. production of, E56
Electromagnet, F25
Electromagnetism, F30–31
Electron, F30
Electronic scale, F52
Elephants
    African, A3, A43
    changes over time, C43
Elliptical orbit, D72
El Niño, D26
ELVES, D25

Embryo, plant, A20
Emergencies, safety in, R18–21
Endangered species, B48–49
Energy, E42
  chemical, E28
  kinetic, E42
  light, E100
  potential, E28
  released by earthquake, C15
  thermal, E56–57
Energy pyramid, B22
Entomologist, A63
**Environmental Protection
  Agency (EPA),** B72–73
Environments, A40
  plant adaptations for, A74
Epicenter, C15
Equator, B28
Erosion, waves and, D41
Eruptions, C18–19, C22–25
Esophagus, A111–112, R30
Estuary, B12
Euglena, A9
Europa, D74
European goldfinch, A48
Evacuation, B56
Evaporation, D34, E27
  humidity and, D21
  in water cycle, D34
Eyelid, R29
Eyes
  caring for, R24
  corrective lenses for, E114

F

Faraday, Michael, F31
Fastball, F38
Fault, C14
Feathers, bird, A49
Femur, A99, R26
Ferrets, black-footed, B48
Fiber optics, E115
Fibrous roots, A79
Fibula, A99, R26
Field geology technician, C27
Filtering, R35
Finches, A48
Fire
  brush, B57
  forest, B50, B55–56

  safety, R18
Fireworks, E24
First aid
  for bleeding, R21
  for burns, R22
  for choking, R20
  for insect bites and stings, R23
  for nosebleeds, R22
  for skin rashes from plants, R23
Fish
  fossil of, C49
  gray snapper, B13
  largest, A3
  porcupine, A50
  scales of, B3
Fish ladders, B62
Fixed pulley, F78
Flexors, R28
Flooding, B54, D3
Florida
  natural wetlands in, B65
Flowers, A22
  healthy, A72
  seeds in, A84
Focus, earthquake, C15
Food
  animals' need for, A42
  bird beaks and, A46–47
  safe preparation of, R10–11
  serving size, R9
Food chains, B21
Food Guide Pyramid, R8
Food web, B23
Footprints, dinosaur, C33
Force(s), F46
  adding, F50
  changing motion, F48
  changing speed, F49
  effort, F70–71, F74, F78–79,
    F85, F88
  friction as, F58
  gravity as, F56
  levers and, F72
  measuring, F51–52
  pushes and pulls, F46
  resulting, F70–71, F74,
    F78–79, F85, F88
  on sliding box, F54–55
  starting motion, F47
  weight, F57
  work and, F74

Forest, pine, B20
**Forest ecosystem, replanting
  trees in,** B63
**Forest edge ecosystem, food
  chain in,** B21
Forest fires, B50, B55–56
Fossil fuel, C52
Fossils, C36
  animal tracks, C40–41
  dinosaur, C32, C40, C44,
    C58–59
  formation of, C36–39
  history of, C58
  importance of, C44
  making, C34–35
  shell, C36
  trace, C37
  track, C37
Foxes, A43
Frame of reference, F41
Franklin, Benjamin, E115, F30
Freezing points (chart), E38
Fresh water, from salt water,
  D32–33
**Freshwater ecosystem, food
  chain in,** B21
Friction, F47, F58
  bicycle and, F58–59
  car brakes and, F37
  gecko feet and, F37
  inclined plane and, F85
  in-line skating and, F58
  snowboarder and, F54
Frogs, B10
Front, D14
Fruit-bearing plants, A22–23
Fruits, A18–19, A22
Fuel, E56
  burning, E56
Fulcrum, F70–71, F74
Fulton, Robert, F90
Fungi, A26
  lichens, A28–29
  molds, A28
  mushrooms, A26–27
  in soil, A2
  structure of, A26–27

Gagarin, Yuri, D87
Galápagos Islands, A48
Galileo (Galilei), D90–91, E115
Galileo, D88
Galle, Johann, D91
Gas, E8
Gas giants, D78
Gastrocnemius, R29
Geckos, F37
Genetic engineer, A89
Germinate, A84
Gesner, Konrad von, C58
Giant clam, B30
Giant river otter, B29
Giant sequoia, A69
Ginkgoes, C43
Giraffes, A42
Glaciers, C43
Gnomon, E101
Gold, density of, E3
Gombe Stream Game Preserve, A64
Gomphotherium, C42
Goodall, Jane, A64
Graduate, R5
Grafting, A86
Grand Canyon, B75
Grant, Ulysses S., B75
Grass, growth of, B8
Gravity, D42
   as force, F56
   snowboarder and, F54
Gray fox, A43
Gray snapper, B13
Gray whales, A58
Great blue heron, B12
Great Red Spot, D78
Greenhouse effect, D12, E56
Ground squirrel, A59
Grouper, B31
Gypsy moth caterpillars, B25

Habitats, B20
   coral reef, B30–32
   loss of, B48
Hale-Bopp comet, D71

Half Dome, B72
Hamstring, A99, R29
Hand lens, R2
Hawai'i
   Keck Observatory in, D85
   volcanoes in, C24
Hawk, A49
Hawkes, Graham, D54–55
Heart, human, A99, A105–106, R32
Heart muscle, A96, A99, R29
Heat, E48
Hedgehog, A51
Herschel, Caroline, D90
Herschel, William, D90
Hertz, Heinrich, F31
Hibernation, A59
Himalayas, C4
Honey mushroom, A3
House finch, A48
Hubble Space Telescope (HST), D86
Human-powered vehicles (HPVs), high-speed, F60–61
Humans
   body structures, A98
   cell replacement in, A94
   circulatory system in, A105
   ecosystems and, B56, B60–65
   intestines of, A95
   respiratory system in, A104
   sound and hearing of, E67
Humerus, A99, R26
Humidity, D21
Hummingbird, A36
Humpback whale, A60–61
Hunting, B48
Hurricane(s), B54, B56
   rating scale, D3
   safety, R19
   storm surges during, D41
Hygrometer, D21
Hyphae, A27

Ice
   density of, E3
   melting of all world's, E3
   skating on, F36
Ice Age, C43

Iceland, C3
Igneous rocks, C48
Iguana, A51
Inclined planes, F82, F84–85
Indiana Dunes, B44
Indian Ocean, D31
Indonesian volcanoes
   Colo, C24
   Krakatau, E66
Infrared radiation, E52
Inner core, Earth's C7
Inner planets, D76–77
Inputs, B7
Insects, A16
Instincts, A56
Insulator, F13
Internet safety, R15
Intertidal zone, B36
Intestines, A95, A111–113, R30–31
Inventors, E62, F92
Invertebrates, A16
Involuntary muscles, R29
Io, D80
Iron
   density of, E3
   freezing and boiling point of, E38
   molten, E39

Jackrabbit, A36
Jackson, Shirley Ann, E34
Japan
   Mount Fuji volcano, C21, C23
   Tokyo earthquake, C28
   Unzen volcano, C24
Jones, Frederick McKinley, E62
Juniper, A21
Jupiter
   discovery of moons, D90
   distance from sun, D69, D71
   moons of, D74, D80, D88
   as outer planet, D78
   in solar system, D70
   tilt of, D61
   weight on (chart), F57

K – L

Kanamori, Hiroo, C28
Kangaroo rat, A40
Kayaks, F90-91
Keck telescope, D85
Kinetic energy, E42
Koala, A44–45
Krakatau volcano, E66
Lambeosaur, C32
Large intestine, A111, A113, R30–31
Lasers, E114–115
Lava, C20–21
Lead, density of, E3
Leaves, function of, A78
Legs, bones and muscles in, A99
Lenses, E114
Leverrier, Urbain, D91
Levers, F70
  boat oar, F68
  broom, F71
  experimenting with, F68–69
  forces and, F72
  lengths of (chart), F66
  parts of, F70–72
  in piano, F73
  in pliers, F73
  seesaw, F72
  in tools, F73
  wheelbarrow, F71
Liana, B33
Lichens, A28–29, B24
Life cycle, plant, A84
Light
  bending, E104
  bouncing, E102–103
  color and, E110–113
  as energy, E100
  laser, E114–115
  optics and, E114–115
  plants and, A70–71
  shadows and, E101
  stopping, E106
  travel of, E98–99
  using, E100
  white, E110
Light bulb, temperature inside, E39
Light microscope, R3

Lightning
  blue jets, D25
  forest fires and, B54
  frequency of, D2
  temperature of, E39
Lignite, C55
Limestone, C36
  fern fossil in, C48
Liquids, E7
  measuring, R5
Liver, R30
Living things
  cells in, A6
  distances traveled by, B2
  in ecosystems, B20–25
  fossils and changes of, C42–43
  homes and roles of, B18–19
  See also Animals; Plants
Lodestone, F30
Loma Prieta earthquake, C15
Loudness, E78
Lungs, A104–106, R34–35

Machines. *See* Simple machines
Mag-lev train, F31
Magma, C20
  chamber, C21
Magnet, F18
  electromagnet, F25
  lodestone as, F30
  poles of, F18
  temporary, F25
Magnetic field, F19
Magnetic pole, F18
Magnetism, history of, F30–31
Magnolia pod fossil, C48
Maiman, T. H., E115
Mammals
  caring for young, A44
  ocean, A41
Mangrove swamps, B14–15
Mangrove trees, B12–13
Mantle, C6
***Manual of Grasses, The* (Chase),** A90
Mariana Trench, D31, D54
Marine biologist, D56
Mars
  Deimos, D80

  distance from sun, D69, D71
  as inner planet, D76–77
  Olympus Mons volcano, D77
  Phobos, D81
  Sojourner probe, D88
  tilt of, D61
  weight on (chart), F57
Martinique
  Mount Pelée volcano on, C21
Mass, E6
Matter, E6
Maxwell, James Clerk, F31
Mealworms, A38–39
Measurement systems, R6
Medical physicist, A116
Medicines from rain forest, B32–33
Mercalli scale, C16–17
Mercury (element)
  density of, E3
  freezing and boiling point of, E38
Mercury (planet)
  distance from sun, D69, D71
  as inner planet, D76–77
  planet year of, D72
  tilt of, D61
  weight on (chart), F57
Mesosphere, D8
Metamorphosis, A44
Meteorologist, D20, D25
Meterstick, R5
Metric measures, R6
Microbiologist, A32
Microorganisms, A9–10
Microrobots, A63
Microscope
  invention of, E115
  light, R3
  using, R3
  viewing cells with, A7–8
Mid-ocean ridge, D50
Migration, A57
Mildew, A28
Mimicry, A52
Minerva Terrace hot springs, B74
Mir, D87

Mirror, E102–103
Mitochondria, A7–8
Mold
  fossil, C38
  fungus, A28
Molting, A44
Monarch butterfly
  instincts of, A56
  migration of, A57
  travel of, A54–55
Moody, Pliny, C33
Moon (of Earth)
  craters on, D61, D84
  distance from Earth, D62
  orbit of, D64–65
  phases of, D64–65
  tides and, D42, D43 (chart)
  weight on, F57
Moon rover, D82
Moray eel, B26
Morel, A27
Morpho butterfly, B29
Motion, F40
  changing, F48
  relative, F41
  speed and, F42–43
  starting, F47
Motor nerves, R36
Mount Everest, D31
Mount Fuji, C21, C23
Mount Mazama, C22
Mount Pelée volcano, C21, C24
Mount Pinatubo volcano, C24
Mount St. Helens volcano,
  C24–25
Mount Spurr, C26–27
Mount Vesuvius, C21, C23
Mouse, B2
Mouth, R30, R34
Movable pulley, F78
MRI machine, F2, F31
Mulberry trees, A78
Muscle(s)
  cardiac, A100–101
  smooth, A99–100
  striated, A100
  tissues, A96–97
Muscular system, A99, R28–29
Mushroom
  cells of, A26
  chanterelle, A27

  honey, A3
  life cycle of, A27
  morel, A27
  poisonous, A24

**National Aeronautics and Space
  Administration (NASA),**
  D26, F62
National forests, B72
**National Oceanic and Atmos-
  pheric Administration
  (NOAA),** D26
National parks
  history of, B74–75
  list of, B72
  Petrified Forest, C39
  using, B66–67
National Parks Service (NPS),
  B44, B74–75
National Trails System Act, B75
Natural gas, C53
Neap tides, D43
Near-shore zone, B36
Neptune
  discovery of, D91
  distance from sun, D69, D71
  as outer planet, D78–79
  tilt of, D61
  weight on (chart), F57
Nerves, A111
Nervous system, A110–111,
  R36-37
Neuron, A110
New Madrid earthquake, C3
Newton, Sir Isaac, E115
Newton (N), F51, R4
Niche, B21
**Nitrogen, freezing and boiling
  point of,** E38
North African ostrich, A3
North American bats, A59
Northern Hemisphere, D66–67
North Pole
  Earth's axis and, D65
  ocean water near, D37
Nose, R25, R34
Nuclear reactor, E34
Nucleus, cell, A7–8
Nutrients, A72

Nutrition, R8

Observatory, D85
Ocean(s)
  currents, D44–45
  depth of, D30–31
  exploring, D54–55
  floor, features of, D50–51
  size of, D31
  tides, D42
  waves, D40–41
Ocean water, D34–37
  content of (chart), D36
Ochoa, Ellen, F62
Octopus, A12, B31
Oersted, Hans, F31
Olympus Mons, D77
Onnes, Heike, F31
Opaque, E106
Open-ocean zone, B36
Optical telescopes, D84
Optics
  history of, E115
  light and, E114–115
Orbit, D65
  elliptical, D72
Organs, A98
Osprey, A49, B64
Ostriches, A3, A36
Outer core, Earth's, C7
Outer planets, D78–79
Owen, Richard, C58
Oxygen
  animals' need for, A41
  in atmosphere, D6
  freezing and boiling point of,
    E38
  heart, lungs, and, A106–107
  human respiratory system
    and, A104–105
  mountain climbers and, D4–5
  photosynthesis and, A73, D7

Pacific Ocean
  Mariana Trench, D31, D54
  size of, D31
Palissy, Bernard, C59

Parallel circuit, F14
Paramecium, A9
Parashant National Monument, AZ, B75
Paricutín, C2
Parrotfish, B30
Pathfinder, D88
Peach tree, A22
Peat, C55
Pelvis, A99, R26–27
Penguins, A44, A49
Penicillium, A28
Penny, changes in, E4
Peregrine falcon, A36
Petrified Forest National Park, C39
Petroleum, C53
Phases, of moon, D64
Phobos, D81
Photocopiers, F3
Photosynthesis, A73, D7, E100
Physical activity, R12
Physical changes, E26–27, E30
Physicist, E34
Piano, levers in, F73
Pike, Dr. Leonard M., A89
Pine forest, organisms in, B20
Pine trees, A21
  bristlecone, A69
  fire and, B55
  white, A21
Piranha, B29
Pistil, A85
Pitch, E79
Planets, D71
  discovering, D90–91
  distances between, D74–75
  distances from sun (chart), D69
  inner, D76–77
  movement of, D68–69
  order from sun (chart), D76
  outer, D78–79
  tilts of (chart), D61
  weight on (chart), F57
Planet years (chart), D72
Plant cells, A8
Plants
  adaptations of, A74, A80
  basic needs of, A72
  "breathing" of, A76–77
  cone-bearing, A20–21

  food for, A73
  fruit-bearing, A22–23
  leaves of, A78
  life cycles of, A84–87
  light and, A70–71
  light energy and, E100
  new from old, A86
  with seeds, A20–23
  skin rashes from, R23
  in tropical rain forests, B32
Platelets, R33
Plates, Earth's, C8, C20
Pliers, levers in, F73
Pluto
  discovery of, D91
  distance from sun, D69, D71
  first detailed photos of, D91
  as outer planet, D78–79
  planet year of, D72
  tilt of, D61
  weight on (chart), F57
Polar bears, A50
Pollination, A85
Pollutants, microbes and, A32
Pollution, B48, B57–58
Polo, Marco, E114
Polyps, B30
Pond
  changes in, B50–51
  pollution of, B57–58
  waves in, E72
Population, B13
Porcupine fish, A50
Position, F40
Posture, at computer, R14
Potato tubers, A87
Potential energy, E28
Prairie dogs, B24
Precipitation, D35
Preservation, B72
Prisms, E110–112
Producers, B21
Prominences, D70
Propellers, F90
Protoceratops, C40
Pull, F46, F51
Pulley, F76-79
Pumpkin seeds, A23
Pupa, A44
Push, F46, F49–50

Q – R

Quadriceps, A99, R28
Queen Mary, F91
Radiation, E52
  infrared, E53
Radioactivity in fossils, C59
Radioimmunoassay (RIA) test, A116
Radio telescopes, D84–85
Radius, A99, R26
Rain, D18
Rainbow, E108–109
Raindrops, as prisms, E111
Rain-forest orchid, B29
Rain forests
  destruction of, B61
  tropical, B28–29
  See also Tropical rain forests
Ramp, F84. *See also* Inclined planes
Raspberry bushes, A82
Reclamation, B63
  strip-mine, B62–63
Recycling
  to reduce trash, B69
  symbol for, B69
  tires, B49
Red blood cells, A95, R33
Redesign, B71
Red fire sponge, A14
Red mangrove tree, B12
Red sprite, D24
Reflecting telescope, D84
Reflection, E102–103
Refracting telescope, D84
Refraction, E104–105
Relative motion, F41
Resistor, F13
Resources
  conservation of, B68–73
  from tropical rain forests, B32
Respiratory system, A104–105, R34–35
Resulting force
  with inclined plane, F85
  with lever, F70–71, F74
  with pulley, F78–79

with screw, F86
with wedges, F88
with wheel and axle, F80
Revolution, Earth's, D65
Rib cage, A99, R26
Richter scale, C16
Ride, Sally, F62
River turtle, B29
Roaches, robot, A62–63
Robins, sound and hearing of,
  E67
Robot ants and roaches, A62–63
Robot volcano explorer, C26–27
Rocks, age of, C48
Roots, underwater mangrove,
  B15
Rose hip, A22
Rotating-drum barometer, D20
Rotation, Earth's, D65, D72
Rotifers, A10
Ruler, using, R5
Rust, E29

S

Safety
  bicycle, R16–17
  earthquake, R19
  fire, R18
  Internet, R15
  storm, R19
Saffir-Simpson Hurricane
  Scale, D3
Saguaro cactus, A69
Salinity, B30
Salmon, B62
  bear catching, A42
  migration of, A58
Salt water
  fresh water from, D32–33
  ocean water as, D36–37
Saltwater crocodile, A3
San Andreas fault, C14
Sandstone, C36
Satellite, D64, F56
Satellite photograph, D22
Saturn
  distance from sun, D69, D71
  as outer planet, D78
  rings around, D80
  tilt of, D61

Titan, D80
weight on (chart), F57
Sayler, Gary, A32
Scale
  dial spring, F52
  electronic, F52
  large, F53
  spring, F51–52, R4
Science tools, using, R2–5
Screws, F86–87
Scuba support crew, D55
Sea Around Us, The (Carson),
  D56
Sea fan, B31
Seahorse, A37
Seashore ecosystem, B43
Seasons, D66
Sea urchin, B30
Sedimentary rocks, C36, C44
Seedlings
  growth of, A82–83
  in mangrove swamp, B14
Seeds
  plants with, A20–23, A84
  watermelon, A18
Seesaw, F72
Seismograph, C16
Seismologist, C28
Sense organs, caring for, R24–25
Sensors, A63
Sensory nerves, R36
Series circuit, F14
Serving size, R9
Shadows, light and, E101
Shale, C36
Sharks, whale, A3
Shelter, animals' need for, A43
Shield volcanoes, C21
Shore zone, D49
Shoulder muscles, A99
Shrimp, B12
Silent Spring (Carson), D56
Silver, tarnishing of, E28
Simple machines, F70
  inclined planes, F84–85
  lever, F68–74
  pulley, F76–79
  screw, F86–87
  water transportation and,
    F90–91
  wedges, F88

wheel and axle, F76, F80
Skeletal muscle, A96
Skeletal system, A98–99
  bones in, R26
  caring for, R27
Skeleton
  bat, A17
  coral polyp, B30–31
  human. *See also* Skeletal system
Skin, caring for, R25
Skin adhesive, A114–115
Skull, R26–27
Small intestine, A111–112,
  R30–31
Smooth muscle, A96, A100
Snails, A15, B21
Snowshoe hare, A52
Sodium chloride, D36
Soil
  bacteria in, A2, B21
  fungi in, A2
  nutrients in, A72
Sojourner probe, D88
Solar energy, E57
Solar system, D70
  asteroids, D71
  comets, D71
  planets, D71
  sun, D70
Solid, E6
Solubility, E19
Solution, E18
Sonic boom, E88
Sound
  ranges of (chart), E67
  speed of, E84
  wave, defined, E71
  wave diagram, E73
  waves, E72–73
Southern Hemisphere, D66
South Pole
  Earth's axis and, D65
  ocean water near, D37
Space exploration
  crewed missions, D87
  space probes, D88–89
  space station, D87
  telescopes and, D84–86
Species
  competition among, B48
  endangered, B48–49

Speed, F42–43
  acceleration and, F48
  of activities (chart), F42
  changing, F49
  of sound, E84
Spider, A16
Spider plant, A86
Spider web, B18
Spinal cord, A111, R36
Spine, A99, R26–27
Spiral staircase, F87
Sponges
  cells of, A14
  living and harvested, B32
  real versus artificial, A12–13
  red fire, A14
  as simplest animals, A14
Spores
  fungi, A24–25, A27
  plants, A85
Spring scale, F51–52, R4
Spring tides, D43
Sprites, D25
Stability, B8
Staghorn coral, B31
Stamen, A85
Star, D70
Starfish, D42
Static electricity, F30
Stationary front, D14
Steel, making, E30
Stems, vine, A74
Stephenson-Hawk, Denise, D26
Stomach
  human, A111–112, R30
  whale, A95
Stonehenge, D68
Stopwatch, F42, R5
Storms
  ecosystems and, B54
  safety in, R19
Storm surge, D41
Stratosphere, D8
Stratus cloud, D15
Striated muscles, A100
Strip-mine reclamation, B62–63
Succession, B52
Sugar, forms of, E27
Sun
  air and, D12
  distance from Earth, D60

  gravity between Earth and, F56
  infrared radiation of, E53
  planets' distance from (chart), D69
  planets in order from (chart), D76
  planets' paths around, D72
  shadows and, E101
  in solar system, D70
Sunspots, D70
Superconductors, F31
Superveggies, A88–89
Surface current, D44
Surgical nurse, A115
Swamp, B13
System(s), B6
  characteristics of, B6–9
  fishbowl as, B4
  human, A98
  interaction in, B4–5, B7
  parts of, B6
  stability and change in, B8
Système International (SI) measures, F51, R6

T

Taproot, A79
Telescopes, D82–86
Temperatures
  in atmosphere, D8
  daily (chart), D22
  land versus water, D20
  of light bulb, E39
  of lightning, E39
  of water in coral reef, B30
Texas, Glen Rose, C37
Thales, F30
Theophrastus, C58
Thermal energy, E56
Thermometer, using, R2
Thermosphere, D8
Thunderstorms
  along cold front, D14
  effect on ecosystems, B54
  frequency of, D2
  unusual flashes during, D24–25
  warning sirens for, B56
  See also Lightning
Tibia, A99, R26
Tide pool, D42

Tides, D42–43
Tiger centipede, B29
Tigers, A38, A60
Timing device, using, R5
Tissue, A98
Titan, D80
Tokyo, earthquake damage in, C28
Tombaugh, Clyde, D91
Tongue, caring for, R25
Tornadoes
  safety and, R19
  sirens for, B56
Tortoise, A37, A40
Toucan, B29
Touch, A108–109
Trace fossils, C37
Trachea, A104–105, R35
Tracks, fossilized, C37
Translucent, E106
Transparent, E106
Transpiration, A78
Trees
  American holly, A22
  cork, A6
  giant sequoia, A69
  peach, A22
  planting, B64
  replanting, B63
  tagged, B72
Trench, ocean, D50
Triceps, A99–100, R28–29
Trieste, D54
Tropical ecosystems, B28–33
Tropical rain forests, B28–29
  resources from, B32
  See also Rain forests
Troposphere, D8
Tubers, A87
Tulips, A86
Tyrannosaurus rex, C59
Tyrrell Museum, Alberta, C32

U

Ulna, A99, R26
Ultimate Bike, F61

Under the Sea-Wind (Carson), D56
Unzen volcano, C24
U.S. Bureau of Fisheries, D56
U.S. Department of Agriculture, A90
U.S. Nuclear Regulatory Commission (NRC), E34
Urania Observatory, D91
Uranus
 discovery of, D90–91
 distance from sun, D69, D71
 as outer planet, D78–79
 tilt of, D61
 weight on (chart), F57

V

Vacuoles, A7–8
Vegetables, A88–89
Veins, A105–106, R32
Vent, C20
Venus
 distance from sun, D69, D71
 as inner planet, D76
 tilt of, D61
 weight on (chart), F57
Venus' flytrap, A80–81
Vertebrates, A16
Viceroy butterfly, A52
Vinegar, E29
Vines, A74
 liana, B33
Vise, F86
Visible spectrum, E110
Volcanoes, C20
 Antarctic, C26–27
 building effects of, C22
 cinder cone, C21
 composite, C21
 destruction from, C24
 eruptions of, C18–19,
  C22–C25, E66
 eruption warnings, B56
 formation of, C20
 in Iceland, C3
 on Mars, D77
 rapid ecosystem changes and,
  B55
 shield, C21
 vent, C20

Volt, F12
Volta, Alessandro, F30–31
Voltaic pile, F30–31
Volume, E13
Voluntary muscles, R29
Volvox, A10
Voyager 2, D89, D91
Vulture, A40

Walking stick, A52–53
Warm front, D14
Water
 animals' need for, A43
 conservation measures (chart),
  B68
 density of, E3
 evaporation, D21
 ocean, D34–37
 plants' need for, A70, A72
 temperatures in coral reef, B30
Water currents, D38–39
Water cycle, D34–35
 in a yard, B6–7
Water ecosystem, B12
 human wastes in, B61
Waterlily, A74
Watermelon, A18
Water transportation, F90–91
Water vapor
 in atmosphere, D6
 in water cycle, D34
Wavelength, E72
Waves
 ocean, D40–41
 pond, E72
 sound, E72–73
Weather
 air and, D12–17
 mapping and charting, D22–23
 measuring, D20–21
 predicting, D20–23
Weather map, D22–23
Wedges, F88
Weekly activities, planning, R12
Weight, F57
Wetlands
 in Florida, B65
 flow control device for, B65
Whale, A41

 blue, A3
 gray, A58
 humpback, A60–61
 stomach of, A95
Whale sharks, A3
Wheel and axle, F76, F80
Wheelbarrow, F67, F71
White blood cells, R33
White light, E110
White mulberry, A78
White pine, A21
Wild and Scenic Rivers Act, B75
Wild orchids, A76
Wilson, Woodrow (President),
 B75
Wind
 speed of, D10–11
 water waves from, D40
Wind pipe, R34
Wind scale (chart), D11
Windsock, D21
Winter storm safety, R19
Wizard Island, C22
Wolves, B2
Woolly mammoths, C43
Work, F74
Workout, guidelines for, R13
Worms, A15, C37
Wright, Orville, F92
Wright, Wilbur, F92
Yalow, Rosalyn Sussman, A116
Yard
 as ecosystem, B10–11
 season changes and, B8–9
 water cycle in, B6–7
Yeasts, A28
Yellowstone National Park, B54
 establishment of, B74
 Minerva Terrace hot springs,
  B74
Yosemite National Park, B72,
 B74–75

J.F. Maxwell/Falls of the Ohio State Park; C64 (b) Sandy Felsenthal/Corbis.

Unit D

Unit D Opener (fg) Dorling Kindersley; (bg) FPG International; D2-D3 Warren Faidley/International Stock; D3 (t) Bob Abraham/The Stock Market; D3 (b) NRSC Ltd/Science Photo Library/Photo Researchers; D4 Keren Su/Stock, Boston; D6 Space Frontiers-TCL/Masterfile; D10 Bruce Watkins/Earth Scenes; D12 Peter Menzel/Stock, Boston; D14-D15 C. O'Rear/Corbis; D15 Warren Faidley/International Stock; D16 (b) Bill Binzen/The Stock Market; D18 J. Taposchaner/FPG International; D20 Sam Ogden/Science Photo Library/Photo Researchers; D21 (t) Breck P. Kent/Earth Scenes; D21 (b) B. Daemmrich/The Image Works; D22 (c) 1998 Accu Weather; D24 Geophysical Institute, University of Alaska, Fairbanks/NASA; D25 Pat Lanza/Bruce Coleman, Inc.; D26 (t) Clark Atlanta University; D26 (b) NASA/Science Photo Library/Photo Researchers; D30-D31 Warren Bolster/Stone; D31 (t) Warren Morgan/Corbis; D31 (b) Tom Van Sant, Geosphere Project/Planetary Visions/Science Photo Library/Photo Researchers; D32 Philip A. Savoie/Bruce Coleman, Inc.; D36 (tr) A. Ramey/Stock Boston; D36 (bl) Richard Gaul/FPG International; D38 John Lel/Stock, Boston; D40 E.R. Degginger/Photo Researchers; D41 (t) Fredrik Bodin/Stock, Boston; D41 (b) Peter Miller/Photo Researchers; D42 (t), D42 (c) Francois Gohier/Photo Researchers; D42 (b) Steinhart Aquarium/Tom McHugh/Photo Researchers; D46 Ralph White/Corbis; D49 (i) Dr. E.R. Degginger/Color-Pic; D49 (t) David R. Frazier; D50-D51 Marie Tharp/Oceanic Cartographer; D54-D55 Ben Margot/AP Photo/Wide World Photos; D55 Thomas Ives/The Stock Market; D56 (t) Erich Hartmann/Magnum Photos; D56 (b) Ron Sefton/Bruce Coleman, Inc.; D60-D61 Ton Kinsbergen/ESA/Science Photo Library/Photo Researchers; D61 NASA; D62 Dr. E. R. Degginger/Color-Pic; D68 Tom Till; D71 Frank Zullo/Photo Researchers; D72-D73 M. Agliolo/Photo Researchers; D74 NASA; D77 (t) U.S. Geological Survey/Science Photo Library/Photo Researchers; D77 (b) David Crisp and the WFPC2 Science Team (Jet Propulsion Laboratory/California Institute of Technology)/NASA; D77 (tc) NASA; D77 (bc) National Oceanic and Atmospheric Administration; D78 NASA; D78-D79 Erich Karkoschka (University of Arizona Lunar & Planetary Lab) and NASA; D79 (r) Dr. R. Albrecht, ESA/ESO Space Telescope European Coordinating Facility, NASA; D79 (c) Lawrence Sromovsky (University of Wisconsin - Madison), NASA; D80, D81, D82 NASA; D84 (r) Michael Freeman; D84 (tl) David Nunuk/Science Photo Library/Photo Researchers; D84 (bl) Omikron Collection/Photo Researchers; D85 (t) Simon Fraser/Science Photo Library/Photo Researchers; D85 (b) Robert Frerck/Stone; D85 (ti) Roger Ressmeyer/Corbis; D86 (bg) Shahn Kermani/Liaison International; D86, D87, D88, D89 NASA; D90 (r) Jean-Loup Charmet; D90 (l) NASA; D91 (t) The Granger Collection, New York; D91 (c) Sylvester Allred/Visuals Unlimited; D91 (b) Mark E. Gibson/Dembinsky Photo Associates; D92 J. Kelly Beatty; D92 (bg) Science VU/Visuals Unlimited; D96 (t) Mark E. Gibson; D96 (b) W. Metzen/H. Armstrong Roberts, Inc..

Unit E

Unit E Opener (fg); Dennis Yankus/Superstock; (bg); Pierre-Yves Goavec/Image Bank; E2-E3 Jon Riley/Stone; E3 Dr. E.R. Degginger/Color-Pic; E4 Superstock; E6 Michael Denora/Liaison International; E8 (b) Bob Abraham/The Stock Market; E10 (l) Lee F. Snyder/Photo Researchers; E14-E15 (b) Richard R. Hansen/Photo Researchers; E16 Stone; E20 (t) Kathy Ferguson/PhotoEdit; E20 (b) Doug Perrine/Innerspace Visions; E20 (bi) Felicia Martinez/PhotoEdit; E21 (b) Chip Clark; E22 (bg) Norbert Wu/Mo Yung Productions; E22-E23 Richard Pasley/Stock, Boston; E24 Stockman/International Stock; E29 (cl) Dr. E.R. Degginger/Color-Pic; E29 (br) Grace Davies; E29 (bl) Index Stock Imagery/PictureQuest; E30 (i) P. Degginger/H. Armstrong Roberts, Inc.; E30 (b) Jack McConnell/McConnell & McNamara; E30-E31 Paul A. Souders/Corbis; E32 Courtesy of J. G.'s Edible Plastic; E33 David R. Frazier; E34 (l) United States Nuclear Regulatory Commission; E34 (r) Tom Carroll/Phototake; E38-E39 Ray Ellis/Photo Researchers; E39 (t) Peter Steiner/The Stock Market; E39 (b) Murray & Assoc./The Stock Market; E40 Craig Tuttle/The Stock Market; E43 (t) Jim Zipp/Photo Researchers; E44 Ted Horowitz/The Stock Market; E48 D. Nabokov/Gamma Liaison; E50 (b) L. West/Bruce Coleman, Inc.; E50 (i) Jonathan Wright/Bruce Coleman, Inc.; E51 Gary Milburn/Tom Stack & Associates; E52 Jeff Foott/Bruce Coleman, Inc.; E56 (t) Craig Hammell/The Stock Market; E56 (b) Russell D. Curtis/Photo Researchers; E57 (tl) Stu Rosner/Stock, Boston; E57 (tr) John Mead/Science Photo Library/Photo Researchers; E57 (br) John Cancalosi/Stock, Boston; E58 (b) David Falconer& Associates; E58 (tr) Telegraph Colour Library/FPG International; E58 (cr) Charles D. Winters/Photo Researchers; E58 (bi) Montes De Oca & Associates; E59 Paul Shambroom/Science Source/Photo Researchers; E61 Danny Daniels/The Picture Cube; E62 Minnesota Historical Society; E62 (i) Peter Vadnai/The Stock Market; E66-E67 Stephen Dalton/Photo Researchers; E67 Carl R. Sams, II/Peter Arnold, Inc.; E68 A. Ramey/PhotoEdit; E71 (b) Summer Productions; E71 (li) Michelle Bridwell/PhotoEdit; E71 (tri) Peter Langone/International Stock; E72 (l) Ian O'Leary/Stone; E76 Randy Duchaine/The Stock Market; E78 (r) Jim Zipp/Photo Researchers; E78 Spencer Grant/PhotoEdit; E82 (t) Bose Corporation; E82 (b) Bose/Lisa Borman Associates; E84-E85 (b) NASA; E90-E91 Bruce Forster/Stone; E91 (i) Jon Riley/Folio; E96-E97 NASA; E97 (i) Chip Simons; E97 (b) David Madison/Bruce Coleman, Inc.; E100 (l) Mark E. Gibson; E100 (r) Bob Daemmrich/Stock, Boston; E103 Jan Butchofsky/Dave G. Houser; E105 (t), 105 (c) Richard Megna/Fundamental Photographs; E108 (b) Randy Duchaine/The Stock Market; E110 Tom Skrivan/The Stock Market; E111 (tr) David Woodfall/Stone; E113 Roy Morsh/The Stock Market; E114-F115 Paul Silverman/Fundamental Photographs; E115 (t) Ed Eckstein/the Franklin Institute Science Museum; E115 (b) Peter Angelo Simon/The Stock Market; E116 (t) Schomburg Collection; E116 (bl) Jim Davie; E120 (t) Sal Dimarco/Black Star; E120 (b) Jack Olson.

Unit F

Unit F Opener (fg) Steve Berman/Liaison International; (bg) Photone Disk #50 ; F2-F3 Pete Saloutos/The Stock Market; F4 Doug Martin/Photo Researchers; F9 Charles D. Winters/Photo Researchers; F10 Cosmo Condina/Stone; F15 Dr. E.R. Degginger/Color-Pic; F16 National Maritime Museum Picture Library; F19

Richard Megna/Fundamental Photographs; F20-F21 (t) Phil Degginger/Color-Pic; F22 Gamma Tokyo/Liaison International; F24-F25 Spencer Grant/PhotoEdit; F25 Tom Pantages; F27 (t), F27 (c) Phil Degginger/Color Pic; F27 (b) Bruno Joachin/Liaison International; F27 (bg) W. Cody/Corbis Westlight; F30 (t) PhotoDisc; F30 (b) Corbis-Bettmann; F31 Phil Degginger/Color-Pic; F32 (i) Fonar Corporation; F32 Jean Miele/The Stock Market; F36-F37 PictureQuest; F37 (t), F37 (ti) Dwight R. Kuhn; F37 (br) Tony Freeman/PhotoEdit; F38 (b) David R. Frazier; F40 (b) Mark E. Gibson; F42 (b) Bob Daemmrich/Stock, Boston; F44 (bl) Miro Vintoniv/Stock, Boston; F46 (bl) Jean-Marc Barey/Agence Vandystadt/Photo Researchers; F47 (tr) Daniel MacDonald/The Stock Shop; F49 Bernard Asset/Agence Vandystadt/Photo Research; F50 (t) Kathi Lamm/Stone; F53 Terry Wild Studio; F54 (b) William R. Sallaz/Duomo Photography; F57 (c) Photo Library International/ESA/Photo Researchers; F57 (cr) Photo Researchers; F58 (bl) Michael Mauney/Stone; F60 (b) Brian Wilson; F60 (t) PA News; F61 (i) Michael Newman/PhotoEdit; F62 (t) UPI/Corbis-Bettmann; F62 NASA; F66-F67 (bg) Dan Porges/Bruce Coleman, Inc.; F67 (tr) R. Sheridan/Ancient Art and Architecture Collection; F67 (tl) The Granger Collection, New York; F68 (bl) William McCoy/Rainbow; F70 (bl) Yoav Levy/Phototake/PictureQuest; F73 (tr) Michael Newman/PhotoEdit; F74 (tr) David R. Frazier; F78 (bl) Mark E. Gibson; F80 (b) Jeff Dunn/Stock, Boston; F82 (bl) Tom King/Tom King, Inc.; F84 (b) Aaron Haupt/David R. Frazier; F85 (tl) Dan McCoy/Rainbow; F85 (br) Michael Newman/PhotoEdit; F85 (cl) David Falconer/Folio; F86 (t) Superstock; F87 (r) Churchill & Klehr; F87 (bl) Staircase & Millwork Corporation, Alpharetta, GA; F88 (br) Tony Freeman/PhotoEdit; F90 (bg) Corel; F90 (l) Archive Photos; F90 (c) Noble Stock/International Stock; F90 (bl) Alexandra Guest/John F. Coates; F91 (l) Eric Sanford/International Stock; F94 (l) Archive Photos; F92 (r) Library of Congress/FPG International; F92 (bl) Library of Congress; F96 (t) Christian Heeb/Gnass Photo Images; F96 (b) Maxine Cass.

Health Handbook: R23 Palm Beach Post; R27 (t) Andrew Spielman/Phototake; (c) Martha McBride/Unicorn Stock; (b) Larry West/FPG International; R28 (l) Ron Chapple/FPG; (c) Mark Scott/FPG; (b) David Lissy/Index Stock.

All other photographs by Harcourt photographers listed below, © Harcourt:
Weronica Ankarorn, Bartlett Digital, Victoria Bowen, Eric Camden, Digital Imaging Group, Charles Hodges, Ken Karp, Ken Kinzie, Ed McDonald, Sheri O'Neal, Terry Sinclair.

Art Credits

Mike Atkinson A85, B22, B23; Jean Calder A99, A100 - 101, A110, A111; Susan Carlson D22; Mike Dammer A33, A65, A91, A117, B45, B77, C29, C61, D27, D57, D93, E35, E63, E93, F117, F33, F63, F93; John Edwards E111; John Francis B14 - 15; Lisa Frasier E56-57; George Fryer C6 - 7, C20, C21, D20; Thomas Gagliano D48 - 49, E73, E78, E79, E80, F14; Patrick Gnan E60, F74; Terry Hadler E14, E19, E49, F78, F79; Tim Hayward C44, C48; Robert Hynes A16, A22, B28 - 29, B30 - 31; Joe LeMoniier A64, A90, E66; Mapquest A57, B40, C46; Janos Marffy D66; Michael Maydak D38 - 39, Sebastian Quigley D12 - 13, D44, D65, D76 - 77, D78 - 79, E6, E7, E8, E22, E72, F6, F7, F20, F24, F56; Eberhard Reinmann A98, A104 - 105, A106, A112, E74; Mike Saunders A7, A8, A20, A26, A27, A73, A84, B52 - 53, C7, C36, D8 - 9, D52 - 53, D70, D71, D72 - 73; Steve Seymour B7, B40 - 41, B62, B63, C8, C9, C10, C15, D14, D43, D86, E43, E44, E51, E52, E70, E85, E88 - 89, F8, F13, F49, F72; Shough E112; Bill Smith Studio D93; Walter Stuart A10 - 11, A14, A15; Steve Weston C14, C22, C23, D15, E72, E86 - 87, F18, F80, F86, F87, F88, F93